INTERPRETATIONS OF POETRY
AND RELIGION

BY GEORGE SANTAYANA

THE LIFE OF REASON: or the Phases of
Human Progress

   I. INTRODUCTION AND REASON IN COMMON SENSE
  II. REASON IN SOCIETY
 III. REASON IN RELIGION
 IV. REASON IN ART
  V. REASON IN SCIENCE

THE SENSE OF BEAUTY

INTERPRETATIONS OF POETRY AND RELIGION

A HERMIT OF CARMEL AND OTHER POEMS

WINDS OF DOCTRINE

CHARACTER AND OPINION IN THE UNITED
STATES   ———

LITTLE ESSAYS DRAWN FROM THE WORKS OF
GEORGE SANTAYANA. By LOGAN PEARSALL
SMITH, with the collaboration of the Author.
12mo.

CHARLES SCRIBNER'S SONS

INTERPRETATIONS

OF

POETRY AND RELIGION

BY

GEORGE SANTAYANA

NEW YORK
CHARLES SCRIBNER'S SONS
1922

PREFACE

THE following volume is composed of a number of papers written at various times and already partially printed; they are now revised and gathered together in the hope that they may lead the reader, from somewhat different points of approach, to a single idea. This idea is that religion and poetry are identical in essence, and differ merely in the way in which they are attached to practical affairs. Poetry is called religion when it intervenes in life, and religion, when it merely supervenes upon life, is seen to be nothing but poetry.

It would naturally follow from this conception that religious doctrines would do well to withdraw their pretension to be dealing with matters of fact. That pretension is not only the source of the conflicts of religion with science and of the vain and bitter controversies of sects; it is also the cause of the impurity and incoherence of religion in the soul, when it seeks its sanctions in the sphere of reality, and forgets that its proper concern is to express the ideal. For the dignity of religion, like that of poetry and of every moral ideal, lies precisely in its ideal adequacy, in its fit rendering of

the meanings and values of life, in its anticipation
of perfection; so that the excellence of religion is
due to an idealization of experience which, while
making religion noble if treated as poetry, makes
it necessarily false if treated as science.   Its function is rather to draw from reality materials for an
image of that ideal to which reality ought to conform, and to make us citizens, by anticipation, in
the world we crave.

It also follows from our general conception that
poetry has a universal and a moral function.   Its
rudimentary essays in the region of fancy and
pleasant sound, as well as its idealization of episodes in human existence, are only partial exercises
in an art that has all time and all experience for
its natural subject-matter and all the possibilities
of being for its ultimate theme.   As religion is
deflected from its course when it is confused with
a record of facts or of natural laws, so poetry is
arrested in its development if it remains an unmeaning play of fancy without relevance to the
ideals and purposes of life.   In that relevance lies
its highest power.   As its elementary pleasantness
comes from its response to the demands of the ear,
so its deepest beauty comes from its response to
the ultimate demands of the soul.

This theory can hardly hope for much commen-
dation either from the apologists of theology or
from its critics.   The mass of mankind is divided

into two classes, the Sancho Panzas who have a
sense for reality, but no ideals, and the Don Quix-
otes with a sense for ideals, but mad. The expe-
dient of recognizing facts as facts and accepting
ideals as ideals, — and this is all we propose, —
although apparently simple enough, seems to elude
the normal human power of discrimination. If,
therefore, the champion of any orthodoxy should
be offended at our conception, which would reduce
his artful cosmos to an allegory, all that could be
said to mitigate his displeasure would be that our
view is even less favourable to his opponents than
to himself.

The liberal school that attempts to fortify religion by minimizing its expression, both theoretic
and devotional, seems from this point of view
to be merely impoverishing religious symbols and
vulgarizing religious aims; it subtracts from faith
that imagination by which faith becomes an interpretation and idealization of human life, and
retains only a stark and superfluous principle of
superstition. For meagre and abstract as may be
the content of such a religion, it contains all the
venom of absolute pretensions; it is no less cursed
than the more developed systems with a controversial unrest and with a consequent undertone of
constraint and suspicion. It tortures itself with
the same circular proofs in its mistaken ambition
to enter the plane of vulgar reality and escape its

native element of ideas. It casts a greater blight
than would a civilized orthodoxy on any joyous
freedom of thought. For the respect exacted by
an establishment is limited and external, and not
greater than its traditional forms probably deserve,
as normal expressions of human feeling and apt
symbols of moral truth. A reasonable deference
once shown to authority, the mind remains, under
such an establishment, inwardly and happily free;
the conscience is not intimidated, the imagination
is not tied up. But the preoccupations of a hungry and abstract fanaticism poison the liberty nomi-
nally allowed, bias all vision, and turn philosophy
itself, which should be the purest of delights and
consolations, into an obsession and a burden to the
soul. In such a spectral form religious illusion
does not cease to be illusion. Mythology cannot
become science by being reduced in bulk, but it
may cease, as a mythology, to be worth having.

On the other hand, the positivistic school of
criticism would seem, if our theory is right, to
have overlooked in its programme the highest
functions of human nature. The environing world
can justify itself to the mind only by the free life
which it fosters there. All observation is observation of brute fact, all discipline is mere repression,
until these facts digested and this discipline embodied in humane impulses become the starting-
point for a creative movement of the imagination,

the firm basis for ideal constructions in society,
religion, and art. Only as conditions of these
human activities can the facts of nature and history become morally intelligible or practically important. In themselves they are trivial incidents,
gossip of the Fates, cacklings of their inexhaustible garrulity. To regard the function of man as
accomplished when these chance happenings have
been recorded by him or contributed to by his
impulsive action, is to ignore his reason, his privilege, — shared for the rest with every living creature, — of using Nature as food and substance for
his own life. This human life is not merely
animal and passionate. The best and keenest
part of it consists in that very gift of creation and
government which, together with all the transcendental functions of his own mind, man has signifi-
cantly attributed to God as to his highest ideal.
Not to see in this rational activity the purpose and
standard of all life is to have left human nature
half unread. It is to look to the removal of certain incidental obstacles in the work of reason as
to the solution of its positive tasks. In comparison
with such apathetic naturalism, all the errors and
follies of religion are worthy of indulgent sympathy,
since they represent an effort, however misguided,
to interpret and to use the materials of experience
for moral ends, and to measure the value of reality
by its relation to the ideal.

The moral function of the imagination and the poetic nature of religion form, then, the theme of the following pages. It may not be amiss to announce it here, as the rather miscellaneous subjects of these essays might at first sight obscure the common import of them all.

CONTENTS

xi

I

UNDERSTANDING, IMAGINATION, AND MYSTICISM

WHEN we consider the situation of the human mind in Nature, its limited plasticity and few channels of communication with the outer world, we need not wonder that we grope for light, or that we find incoherence and instability in human systems of ideas. The wonder rather is that we have done so well, that in the chaos of sensations and passions that fills the mind, we have found any leisure for self-concentration and reflection, and have succeeded in gathering even a light harvest of experience from our distracted labours. Our occasional madness is less wonderful than our occasional sanity. Relapses into dreams are to be expected in a being whose brief existence is so like a dream; but who could have been sure of this sturdy and indomitable perseverance in the work of reason in spite of all checks and discouragements?

The resources of the mind are not commensurate with its ambition. Of the five senses, three are of

little use in the formation of permanent notions:
a fourth, sight, is indeed vivid and luminous, but
furnishes transcripts of things so highly coloured
and deeply modified by the medium of sense, that
a long labour of analysis and correction is needed
before satisfactory conceptions can be extracted
from it.   For this labour, however, we are endowed with the requisite instrument.   We have
memory and we have certain powers of synthesis,
abstraction, reproduction, invention, — in a word,
we have understanding.   But this faculty of understanding has hardly begun its work of decipher-
ing the hieroglyphics of sense and framing an
idea of reality, when it is crossed by another
faculty — the imagination.   Perceptions do not remain in the mind, as would be suggested by the
trite simile of the seal and the wax, passive and
changeless, until time wear off their sharp edges
and make them fade.   No, perceptions fall into
the brain rather as seeds into a furrowed field or
even as sparks into a keg of powder.   Each image
breeds a hundred more, sometimes slowly and sub-
terraneously, sometimes (when a passionate train
is started) with a sudden burst of fancy.   The
mind, exercised by its own fertility and flooded by
its inner lights, has infinite trouble to keep a true
reckoning of its outward perceptions.   It turns
from the frigid problems of observation to its own
visions; it forgets to watch the courses of what

should be its "pilot stars." Indeed, were it not for the power of convention in which, by a sort of mutual cancellation of errors, the more practical and normal conceptions are enshrined, the imagination would carry men wholly away, — the best men first and the vulgar after them. Even as it is, individuals and ages of fervid imagination usually waste themselves in dreams, and must disappear before the race, saddened and dazed, perhaps, by the memory of those visions, can return to its plodding thoughts.

Five senses, then, to gather a small part of the infinite influences that vibrate in Nature, a moderate power of understanding to interpret those senses, and an irregular, passionate fancy to overlay that interpretation — such is the endowment of the human mind. And what is its ambition? Nothing less than to construct a picture of all reality, to comprehend its own origin and that of the universe, to discover the laws of both and prophesy their destiny. Is not the disproportion enormous? Are not confusions and profound contradictions to be looked for in an attempt to build so much out of so little?

Yet the metaphysical ambition we speak of cannot be abandoned, because whatever picture of things we may carry about in our heads we are bound to regard as a map of reality; although we may mark certain tracts of it "unexplored country," the very existence of such regions is vouched for only by our representation, and is necessarily believed to correspond to our idea. All we can do is, without abandoning the aspiration to knowledge which is the inalienable birthright of reason, to control as best we may the formation of our conceptions; to arrange them according to their derivation and measure them by their applicability in life, so prudently watching over their growth that we may be spared the deepest of sorrows — to survive the offspring of our own thought.

The inadequacy of each of our faculties is what occasions the intrusion of some other faculty into its field. The defect of sense calls in imagination, the defect of imagination calls in reasoning, the defect of reasoning divination. If our senses were clairvoyant and able to observe all that is going on in the world, if our instincts were steady, prompting us to adequate reactions upon these observations, the fancy might remain free. We should not need to call upon it to piece out the imperfections of sense and reflection, but we should employ it only in avowed poetry, only in building dream-worlds alongside of the real, not interfering with the latter or confusing it, but repeating its pattern with as many variations as the fertility of our minds could supply. As it is, the imagination is brought into the service of sense and instinct, and made to do the work of intelligence. This substitution is the more readily effected, in that imagination and intelligence do not differ in their origin, but only in their validity. Understanding is an applicable fiction, a kind of wit with a practical use. Common sense and science live in a world of expurgated mythology, such as Plato wished his poets to compose, a world where the objects are imaginative in their origin and essence, but useful, abstract, and beneficent in their suggestions. The sphere of common sense and science is concentric with the sphere of fancy; both move in virtue of the same imaginative impulses. The eventual distinction between intelligence and imagination is ideal; it arises when we discriminate various functions in a life that is dynamically one. Those conceptions which, after they have spontaneously arisen, prove serviceable in practice, and capable of verification in sense, we call ideas of the understanding. The others remain ideas of the imagination. The shortness of life, the distractions of passion, and the misrepresentation to which all transmitted knowledge is subject, have made the testing of ideas by practice extremely slow in the history of mankind. Hence the impurity of our knowledge, its confusion with fancy, and its painful inadequacy to interpret the whole world of human interests. These shortcomings are so many invitations to foreign powers to intervene, so many occasions for new waves of imagination to sweep

away the landmarks of our old labour, and flood
the whole mind with impetuous dreams.

It is accordingly the profounder minds that commonly yield to the imagination, because it is these
minds that are capable of feeling the greatness of
the problems of life and the inadequacy of the
understanding, with its present resources, to solve
them. The same minds are, moreover, often swayed
by emotion, by the ever-present desire to find a
noble solution to all questions, perhaps a solution
already hallowed by authority and intertwined inex-
tricably, for those who have always accepted it,
with the sanctions of spiritual life. Such a coveted
conclusion may easily be one which the understanding, with its basis in sense and its demand for verification, may not be able to reach. Therefore the
impassioned soul must pass beyond the understanding, or else go unsatisfied; and unless it be as disciplined as it is impassioned it will not tolerate
dissatisfaction. From what quarter, then, will it
draw the wider views, the deeper harmonies, which
it craves? Only from the imagination. There is
no other faculty left to invoke. The imagination,
therefore, must furnish to religion and to metaphysics those large ideas tinctured with passion,
those supersensible forms shrouded in awe, in which
alone a mind of great sweep and vitality can find
its congenial objects. Thus the stone which the
builder, understanding, rejected, becomes the chief

stone of the corner; the intuitions which science could not use remain the inspiration of poetry and religion.

The imagination, when thus employed to anticipate or correct the conclusions of the understanding, is of course not called imagination by those who appeal to it. The religious teachers call it prophecy or revelation, the philosophers call it a higher reason. But these names are merely eulogistic synonyms for imagination, implying (what is perfectly possible) that the imagination has not misled us. They imply on the contrary that in the given instances the imagination has hit upon an ultimate truth. A prophet, unless he be the merely mechanical vehicle of truths he does not understand, cannot be conceived as anything but a man of imagination, whose visions miraculously mirror the truth. A metaphysician who transcends the intellect by his reason can be conceived only as using his imagination to such good purpose as to divine by it the ideal laws of reality or the ultimate goals of moral effort. His reason is an imagination that succeeds, an intuition that guesses the principle of experience. But if this intuition were of such a nature that experience could verify it, then that higher reason or imagination would be brought down to the level of the understanding; for understanding, as we have defined it, is itself a kind of imagination, an imagination prophetic of experience, a spontaneity of thought by which the science of perception is turned into the art of life. The same absence of verification distinguishes revelation from science; for when the prophecies of faith are verified, the function of faith is gone. Faith and the higher reason of the metaphysicians are therefore forms of imagination believed to be avenues to truth, as dreams or oracles may sometimes be truthful, not because their necessary correspondence to truth can be demonstrated, for then they would be portions of science, but because a man dwelling on those intuitions is conscious of a certain moral transformation, of a certain warmth and energy of life. This emotion, heightening his ideas and giving them power over his will, he calls faith or high philosophy, and under its dominion he is able to face his destiny with enthusiasm, or at least with composure.

The imagination, even when its premonitions are not wholly justified by subsequent experience, has thus a noble rôle to play in the life of man. Without it his thoughts would be not only far too narrow to represent, although it were symbolically, the greatness of the universe, but far too narrow even to render the scope of his own life and the conditions of his practical welfare. Without poetry and religion the history of mankind would have been darker than it is. Not only would emotional life have been poorer, but the public conscience, the national and family spirit, so useful for moral organization and discipline, would hardly have become articulate. By what a complex and uninspired argumentation would the pure moralist have to insist upon those duties which the imagination enforces so powerfully in oaths sworn before the gods, in commandments written by the finger of God upon stone tablets, in visions of hell and heaven, in chivalrous love and loyalty, and in the sense of family dignity and honour? What intricate, what unavailing appeals to positive interests would have to be made before those quick reactions could be secured in large bodies of people which can be produced by the sight of a flag or the sound of a name? The imagination is the great unifier of humanity. Men's perceptions may be various, their powers of understanding very unequal; but the imagination is, as it were, the self-consciousness of instinct, the contribution which the inner capacity and demand of the mind makes to experience. To indulge the imagination is to express the universal self, the common and contagious element in all individuals, that rudimentary potency which they all share. To stimulate the imagination is to produce the deepest, the most pertinacious emotions. To repress it is to chill the soul, so that even the clearest perception of the truth remains without the joy and impetuosity of conviction.

The part played by imagination is thus indispensable; but obviously the necessity and beneficence of this contribution makes the dangers of it correspondingly great. Wielding a great power, exercising an omnipresent function, the imagination may abuse a great force. While its inspirations coincide with what would be the dictates of reason, were reason audible in the world, all is well, and the progress of man is accelerated by his visions; but being a principle *a priori* the imagination is an irresponsible principle; its rightness is an inward rightness, and everything in the real world may turn out to be disposed otherwise than as it would wish. Our imaginative preconceptions are then obstacles to the perception of fact and of rational duty; the faith that stimulated our efforts and increased our momentum, multiplies our wanderings. The too hasty organization of our thoughts becomes the cause of their more prolonged disorganization, for to the natural obscurity of things and the difficulty of making them fit together among themselves, we add the cross lights of our prejudices and the impossibility of fitting reality into the frame we have made for it in our ignorance of its constitution and extent. And as we love our hopes, and detest the experience that seems to contradict them, we add fanaticism to our confusion. The habits of the imagination, in conflict with the facts of sense, thus come to cloud science with passion, with fiction, with sentimental prejudice. Nor is this the end of our troubles. For Imagination herself suffers violence in this struggle; she seeks to reduce herself to conformity with existence, in the hope of vindicating her nominal authority at the price of some concessions. She begins to feign that she demanded nothing but what she finds. Thus she loses her honesty and freedom, becomes a flatterer of things instead of the principle of their ideal correction, and in the attempt to prove herself prophetic and literally valid (as in a moment of infatuation she had fancied herself to be) she forfeits that symbolic truth, that inner propriety, which gave her a moral value. Thus the false steps of the imagination lead to a contorted science and to a servile ideal.

These complications not unnaturally inspire discouragement and a sense of the hopeless relativity of human thought. Indeed, if there be any special endowment of mind and body called human nature, as there seems to be, it is obvious that all human experience must be relative to that. But the truth, the absolute reality, surrounds and precedes these operations of finite faculty. What value, then, we may say, have these various ideals or perceptions, or the conflicts between them? Are not our senses as human, as "subjective" as our wills? Is not the understanding as visionary as the fancy? Does it not transform the Unknowable into as remote a symbol as does the vainest dream?

The answer which a rational philosophy would make to these questions would be a double one. It is true that every idea is equally relative to human nature and that nothing can be represented in the human mind except by the operation of human faculties. But it is not true that all these products of human ideation are of equal value, since they are not equally conducive to human purposes or satisfactory to human demands.

The impulse that would throw over as equally worthless every product of human art, because it is not indistinguishable from some alleged external reality, does not perceive the serious self-contradictions under which it labours. In the first place the notion of an external reality is a human notion; our reason makes that hypothesis, and its verification in our experience is one of the ideals of science, as its validity is one of the assumptions of daily life. In throwing over all human ideas, because they are infected with humanity, all human ideas are being sacrificed to one of them — the idea of an absolute reality. If this idea, being human, deserved that such sacrifices should be made for it, have the other notions of the mind no rights? Furthermore, even if we granted for the sake of argument a reality which our thoughts were essentially helpless to represent, whence comes the duty of our thoughts to represent it? Whence comes the value of this unattainable truth? From an ideal of human reason. We covet truth. So that the attempt to surrender all human science as relative and all human ideals as trivial is founded on a blind belief in one human idea and an absolute surrender to one human passion.

In spite of these contradictions, which only a dispassionate logic could thoroughly unravel, the enthusiast is apt to rush on. The vision of absolute truth and absolute reality intoxicates him, and as he is too subtle a thinker, too inward a man, to accept the content of his senses or the conventions of his intelligence for unqualified verities, he fortifies himself against them with the consciousness of their relativity, and seeks to rise above them in his meditations. But to rise to what? To some more elaborate idea? To some object, like a scientific cosmos or a religious creed, put together by longer and more indirect processes than those of common perception? Surely not. If I renounce my senses and vulgar intellect because they are infected with finitude and smell of humanity, how shall I accept a work of art, a product of reasoning, or an idol made originally with hands and now encrusted all over, like the statue of Glaucus, with traditional accretions? Poetry, science, and religion, in their positive constructions, are more human, more conditioned, than are the senses and the common understanding themselves. The lover of inviolate reality must not look to them. If the data of human knowledge must be rejected as subjective, how much more should we reject the inferences made from those data by human thought. The way of true wisdom, therefore, if true wisdom is to deal with the Absolute, can only lie in abstention: neither the senses nor the common understanding, and much less the superstructure raised upon these by imagination, logic, or tradition, must delude us: we must keep our thoughts fixed upon the inanity of all this in comparison with the unthinkable truth, with the undivided and unimaginable reality. Everything, says the mystic, is nothing, in comparison with the One.

This confusion, the logical contradiction of which we have just seen, may, for lack of a more specific word, be called mysticism. It consists in the surrender of a category of thought on account of the discovery of its relativity. If I saw or reasoned or judged by such a category, I should be seeing, reasoning, or judging in a specific manner, in a manner conditioned by my finite nature. But the specific and the finite, I feel, are odious; let me therefore aspire to see, reason and judge in no specific or finite manner — that is, not to see, reason or judge at all. So I shall be like the Infinite, nay I shall become one with the Infinite and (marvellous thought!) one with the One.

The ideal of mysticism is accordingly exactly contrary to the ideal of reason; instead of perfecting human nature it seeks to abolish it; instead of building a better world, it would undermine the foundations even of the world we have built already; instead of developing our mind to greater scope and precision, it would return to the condition of protoplasm — to the blessed consciousness of an Unutterable Reality. In the primary stages, of course, mysticism does not venture to abolish all our ideas, or to renounce all our categories of thought. Thus many Christian mystics have still clung, out of respect for authority, to traditional theology, and many philosophical mystics have made some room for life and science in the postscripts which they, like Parmenides, have appended to the blank monism of their systems. But such concessions or hesitations are inconsistent with the mystical spirit which will never be satisfied, if fully developed and fearless, with anything short of Absolute Nothing.

For the very reason, however, that mysticism is a tendency to obliterate distinctions, a partial mysticism often serves to bring out with wonderful intensity those underlying strata of experience which it has not yet decomposed. The razing of the edifice of reason may sometimes discover its foundations. Or the disappearance of one department of activity may throw the mind with greater energy into another. So Spinoza, who combined mysticism in morals with rationalism in science, can bring out the unqualified naturalism of his system with a purity and impressiveness impossible to men who still retain an ideal world, and seek to direct endeavour as well as to describe it. Having renounced all ideal categories, Spinoza has only the material categories left with which to cover the ground. He thus acquires all the concentrated intensity, all the splendid narrowness, which had belonged to Lucretius, while his mystical treatment of the spheres which Lucretius simply ignored, gives him the appearance of a greater profundity. So an ordinary Christian who is mystical, let us say, about time and space, may use his transcendentalism in that sphere to intensify his positivism in theology, and to emphasize his whole-souled surrender to a devout life.

What is impossible is to be a transcendentalist "all 'round." In that case there would be nothing left to transcend; the civil war of the mind would have ended in the extermination of all parties. The art of mysticism is to be mystical in spots and to aim the heavy guns of your transcendental philosophy against those realities or those ideas which you find particularly galling. Planted on your dearest dogma, on your most precious postulate, you may then transcend everything else to your heart's content. You may say with an air of enlightened profundity that nothing is "really" right or wrong, because in Nature all things are regular and necessary, and God cannot act for purposes as if his will were not already accomplished; your mysticism in religion and morals is kept standing, as it were, by the stiff backing which is furnished by your materialistic cosmology. Or you may say with a tone of devout rapture that all sights and sounds are direct messages from Divine Providence to the soul, without any objects "really" existing in space; your mysticism about the world of perception and scientific inference is sustained by the naïve theological dogmas which you substitute for the conceptions of common sense. Yet among these partialities an᾽ blind denials a man's positive insight seems to thrive, and he fortifies and concentrates himself on his chosen ground by his arbitrary exclusions. The patient art of rationalizing the various sides of life, the observational as well as the moral, without confusing them, is an art apparently seldom given to the haste and pugnacity of philosophers.

Thus mysticism, although a principle of dissolution, carries with it the safeguard that it can never be consistently applied. We reach it only in exceptional moments of intuition, from which we descend to our pots and pans with habits and instincts virtually unimpaired. Life goes on; virtues and affections endure, none the worse, the

6

mystic feels, for that slight film of unreality which
envelops them in a mind not unacquainted with
ecstasy.   And although mysticism, left free to
express itself, can have no other goal than Nir-
vana, yet moderately indulged in and duly inhib-
ited by a residuum of conventional sanity, it
serves to give a touch of strangeness and elevation to the character and to suggest superhuman
gifts.   It is not, however, in the least superhuman.   It is hardly even abnormal, being only
an exaggeration of a rational interest in the highest abstractions.   The divine, the universal, the
absolute, even the One, are legitimate conceptions.
They are terms of human thought having as such
a meaning in language and a place in speculation.
Those who live in the mind, whose passions are
only audible in the keen overtones of dialectic,
are no doubt exalted and privileged natures, choos-
ing a better part which should not be taken from
them.   So the poet and the mathematician have
their spheres of abstract and delicate labour, in
which a liberal legislator would not disturb them.
Trouble only arises when the dialectician represents
his rational dreams as knowledge of existences, and
the mystic his excusable raptures as the only way
of life.   Poets and mathematicians do not imagine
that their pursuits raise them above human limitations and are no part of human life, but rather
its only goal and justification.   Such a pretension

would be regarded as madness in the mathematician or the poet; and is not the mystic as miserably a man? Is he not embodying, at his best, the analytic power of a logician, or the imagination of an enthusiast, and, at his worst, the lowest and most obscure passions of human nature?

Yes, in spite of himself, the mystic remains human. Nothing is more normal than abstraction. A contemplative mind drops easily its practical preoccupations, rises easily into an ideal sympathy with impersonal things. The wheels of the universe have a wonderful magnetism for the human will. Our consciousness likes to lose itself in the music of the spheres, a music that finer ears are sometimes privileged to catch. The better side of mysticism is an æsthetic interest in large unities and cosmic laws. The æsthetic attitude is not the moral, but it is not for that reason illegitimate. It gives us refreshment and a foretaste of that perfect adaptation of things to our faculties and of our faculties to things which, could it extend to every part of experience, would constitute the ideal life. Such happiness is denied us in the concrete; but a hint and example of it may be gathered by an abstracted element of our nature as it travels through an abstracted world. Such an indulgence adds to the value of reality only such value as it may itself have in momentary experience; it may have a doubtful moral effect on the happy dreamer

himself. But it serves to keep alive the conviction, which a confused experience might obscure,
that perfection is essentially possible; it reminds
us, like music, that there are worlds far removed
from the actual which are yet living and very near
to the heart. Such is the fruit of abstraction when
abstraction bears any fruit. If the imagination
merely alienates us from reality, without giving
us either a model for its correction or a glimpse
into its structure, it becomes the refuge of poetical
selfishness. Such selfishness is barren, and the
fancy, feeding only on itself, grows leaner every
day. Mysticism is usually an incurable disease.
Facts cannot arouse it, since it never denied them.
Reason cannot convince it, for reason is a human
faculty, assuming a validity which it cannot prove.
The only thing that can kill mysticism is its own
uninterrupted progress, by which it gradually devours every function of the soul and at last, by
destroying its own natural basis, immolates itself
to its inexorable ideal.

Need we ask, after all these reflections, where
we should look for that expansion and elevation of
the mind which the mystic seeks so passionately
and so unintelligently? We can find that expansion, in the first place, in the imagination itself.
That is the true realm of man's infinity, where
novelty may exist without falsity and perpetual
diversity without contradiction. But such exercise

of imagination leaves the world of knowledge untouched. Is there no escape from the prison, as the mystic thinks it, of science and history which shall yet not carry us beyond reality? Is there no truth beyond conventional truth, no life behind human existence?

Certainly. Behind the discovered there is the discoverable, beyond the actual, the possible. Science and history are not exhausted. In their determinate directions they are as infinite as fancy in its indetermination. The spectacle which science and history now spread before us is as far beyond the experience of an ephemeral insect as any Absolute can be beyond our own; yet we have put that spectacle together out of just such sensations as the insect may have — out of this sunlight and this buzz and these momentary throbs of existence. The understanding has indeed supervened, but it has supervened not to deny the validity of those sensations, but to combine their messages. We may still continue in the same path, by the indefinite extension of science over a world of experience and of intelligible truth. Is that prospect insufficient for our ambition? With a world so full of stuff before him, I can hardly conceive what morbid instinct can tempt a man to look elsewhere for wider vistas, unless it be unwillingness to endure the sadness and the discipline of the truth.

But can our situation be made better by refusing to understand it? If we renounced mysticism altogether and kept imagination in its place, should we not live in a clearer and safer world, as well as in a truer? Nay, are we sure that this gradually unfolding, intelligible, and real world would not turn out to be more congenial and beautiful than any wilful fiction, since it would be the product of a universal human labour and the scene of the accumulated sufferings and triumphs of mankind? When we compare the temple which we call Nature, built of sights and sounds by memory and understanding, with all the wonderful worlds evocable by the magician's wand, may we not prefer the humbler and more lasting edifice, not only as a dwelling, but even as a house of prayer? It is not always the loftiest architecture that expresses the deepest soul; the inmost religion of the Pagan haunted his hearth as that of the Christian his catacombs or his hermitage. So philosophy is more spiritual in her humility and abstinence than in her short-lived audacities, and she would do well to inscribe over her gates what, in an ancient Spanish church, may be seen written near the steep entrance to a little subterraneous crypt: —

> "Wouldst thou pass this lowly door?
> Go, and angels greet thee there;
> For by this their sacred stair
> To descend is still to soar.

Bid a measured silence keep
What thy thoughts be telling o'er ;
Sink, to rise with wider sweep
To the heaven of thy rest,
For he climbs the heavens best
Who would touch the deepest deep."

II

THE HOMERIC HYMNS

WE of this generation look back upon a variety of religious conceptions and forms of worship, and a certain unsatisfied hunger in our own souls attaches our attention to the spectacle. We observe how literally fables and mysteries were once accepted which can have for us now only a thin and symbolical meaning. Judging other minds and other ages by our own, we are tempted to ask if there ever was any fundamental difference between religion and poetry. Both seem to consist in what the imagination adds to science, to history, and to morals. Men looked attentively on the face of Nature: their close struggle with her compelled them to do so: but before making statistics of her movements they made dramatizations of her life. The imagination enveloped the material world, as yet imperfectly studied, and produced the cosmos of mythology.

Thus the religion of the Greeks was, we might say, nothing but poetry: nothing but what imagination added to the rudiments of science, to the first impressions of a mind that pored upon natural phenomena and responded to them with a quick sense of kinship and comprehension. The religion of the Hebrews might be called poetry with as good reason. Their "sense for conduct" and their vivid interest in their national destiny carried them past any prosaic record of events or cautious theory of moral and social laws. They rose at once into a bold dramatic conception of their race's covenant with Heaven : just such a conception as the playwright would seek out in order to portray with awful acceleration the ways of passion and fate. Finally, we have apparently a third kind of poetry in what has been the natural religion of the detached philosophers of all ages. In them the imagination touches the precepts of morals and the ideals of reason, attributing to them a larger scope and more perfect fulfilment than experience can show them to have. Philosophers ever tend to clothe the harmonies of their personal thought with universal validity and to assign to their ideals a latent omnipotence and an ultimate victory over the forces of unreason. This which is obviously a kind of poetry is at the same time the spontaneous religion of conscience and thought.

Yet religion in all these cases differs from a mere play of the imagination in one important respect; it reacts directly upon life; it is a factor

in conduct.   Our religion is the poetry in which
we believe.   Mere poetry is an ineffectual shadow
of life; religion is, if you will, a phantom also, but
a phantom guide.   While it tends to its own expansion, like any growth in the imagination, it
tends also to its application in practice.   Such
an aim is foreign to poetry.   The inspirations of
religion demand fidelity and courageous response
on our part.   Faith brings us not only peace, not
only the contemplation of ideal harmonies, but
labour and the sword.   These two tendencies — to
imaginative growth and to practical embodiment
— coexist in every living religion, but they are
not always equally conspicuous.   In the formative
ages of Christianity, for instance, while its legends
were being gathered and its dogma fixed, the imaginative expansion absorbed men's interest; later,
when the luxuriant branches of the Church began
to shake off their foliage, and there came a time
of year

> " When yellow leaves, or none, or few, do hang
> Upon those boughs which shake against the cold,"

the energy of religious thought, released from the
enlargement of doctrine, spent itself upon a more
rigid and watchful application of the residuum of
faith.

In the Pagan religion the element of applicability might seem at first sight to be lacking, so

that nothing would subsist but a poetic fable. An unbiassed study of antiquity, however, will soon dispel that idea. Besides the gods whom we may plausibly regard as impersonations of natural forces, there existed others; the spirits of ancestors, the gods of the hearth, and the ideal patrons of war and the arts. Even the gods of Nature inspired reverence and secured a cultus only as they influenced the well-being of man. The worship of them had a practical import. The conception of their nature and presence became a sanction and an inspiration in the conduct of life. When the figments of the fancy are wholly divorced from reality they can have no clearness or consistency; they can have no permanence when they are wholly devoid of utility. The vividness and persistence of the figures of many of the gods came from the fact that they were associated with institutions and practices which controlled the conception of them and kept it young. The fictions of a poet, whatever his genius, do not produce illusion because they do not attach themselves to realities in the world of action. They have character without power and names without local habitations. The gods in the beginning had both. Their image, their haunts, the reports of their apparitions and miracles, gave a nucleus of empirical reality to the accretions of legend. The poet who came to sing their praise, to enlarge upon their exploits,

and to explain their cultus, gave less to the gods
in honour than he received from them in inspiration. All his invention was guided by the genius
of the deity, as represented by the traditions of
his shrine. This poetry, then, even in its most
playful mood, is not mere poetry, but religion. It
is a poetry in which men believe; it is a poetry
that beautifies and justifies to their minds the
positive facts of their ancestral worship, their
social unity, and their personal conscience.

These general reflections may help us to approach
the hymns of Homer in a becoming spirit. For in
them we find the extreme of fancy, the approach
to a divorce between the imagination and the faith
of the worshipper. Consequently there is danger
that we may allow ourselves to read these lives of
the gods as the composition of a profane poet. If
we did so we should fail to understand not only
their spirit as a whole but many of their parts, in
which notes are struck now of devotion and affec-
tionate pride, now of gratitude and entreaty. These
may be addressed, it is true, to a being that has
just been described as guilty of some signal vice
or treachery, and the contradiction may well stag-
ger a Puritan critic. But the lusts of life were
once for all in the blood of the Pagan gods, who
were the articulate voices of Nature and of passion.
The half-meant exaggeration of a well-known trait
in the divinity would not render the poets that

indulged in it unwelcome to the god; he could feel the sure faith and affection of his worshippers even in their good-humoured laughter at his imaginary plights and naughtiness. The clown was not excluded from these rites. His wit also counted as a service.

The Homeric Hymns, if we may trust the impression they produce on a modern, are not hymns and are not Homer's. They are fragments of narrative in Ionic hexameter recited during the feasts and fairs at various Greek shrines. They are not melodies to be chanted with a common voice by the assemblage during a sacrifice; they are tales delivered by the minstrel to the listening audience of citizens and strangers. They usually have a local reference. Thus we find under the title of a hymn to Apollo a song of Delos and one of Delphi. Delos is a barren rock; its wealth was due to the temple that attracted to the place pilgrimages and embassies, not without rich offerings, from many Greek cities. Accordingly we hear how Leto or Latona, when about to become the mother of Apollo, wandered about the cities and mountains of Greece and Asia, seeking a birthplace for her son. None would receive her, but all the islands trembled at the awful honour of such a nativity, profitable as the honour might eventually prove, —

> " Until at length
> The lovely goddess came to Delos' side

And, making question, spake these wingèd words :
' Delos, were it thy will to be the seat
Of my young son Apollo, brightest god,
And build him a rich fane, no other power
Should ever touch thee or work ill upon thee.
I tell thee not thou shalt be rich in kine
Or in fair flocks, much fruit, or myriad flowers ;
But when Apollo of the far-felt dart
Hath here his shrine, all men will gather here
Bringing thee hecatombs. . . . And though thy soil be poor,
The gods shall make thee strong against thy foes.' "

The spirit of the island is naturally not averse
to so favourable a proposition but, like some too
humble maiden wooed by a great prince, has some
misgivings lest this promise of unexpected good
fortune should veil the approach of some worse
calamity. " When the god is born into the light
of day," she says, " will he not despise me, seeing
how barren I am, and sink me in the sea

> " That ever will
> Oppress my heart with many a watery hill ?
> And therefore let him choose some other land,
> Where he shall please, to build at his command
> Temple and grove set thick with many a tree.
> For wretched polypuses breed in me,
> Retiring chambers, and black sea-calves den
> In my poor soil, for penury of men." [1]

Leto reassures the island, however, and swears
to build a great temple there which her son will
haunt perpetually, preferring it to all his other

[1] Chapman's version.

shrines. Delos consents, and Apollo is born amid
the ministrations of all the goddesses except Hera,
who sits indignant and revengeful in the solitudes
of Olympus. The child is bathed in the stream
and delicately swaddled; but after tasting the nec-
tar and ambrosia which one of the nymphs is quick
to offer him, he bursts his bands, calls for his
bow and his lyre, and flies upward into the sky
announcing that he will henceforth declare the will
of Zeus to mortals. Thereupon —

> "All the immortals stood
> In deep amaze. . . .
> All Delos, looking on him, all with gold
> Was loaded straight, and joy'd to be extoll'd.
> . . . For so she flourished, as a hill that stood
> Crown'd with the flower of an abundant wood." [1]

This legend, with all that accompanies it con-
cerning the glories of Delos and its gods, and the
pilgrimages and games that enlivened the island,
was well-conceived to give form and justification to
the cultus of the temple, and to delight the vota-
ries whom custom or vague instincts of piety had
gathered there. The sacred poet, in another part
of this hymn, does the same service to the even
greater sanctuary of Delphi. He tells us how
Apollo wandered over many lands and waters, and
he stops lovingly to recall the names of the various
spots that claimed the honour of having at some

[1] Chapman's version.

time been visited by the god. The minstrels, wan-
derers themselves, loved to celebrate in this way
the shores they had seen or heard of, and to fill
at the same time their listener's minds with the
spell of sonorous names, the sense of space and
the thrill of mystery. In his journeys Apollo,
the hymn tells us, finally came to the dell and
fountain of Delphusa on the skirts of Parnassus.
The nymph of the spot, fearing the encroachments
of so much more powerful a deity, deceived him
and persuaded him to plant his temple on another
site, where Parnassus fronts the west, and the
overhanging rocks form a cavern. There Apollo
established his temple for the succour and enlightenment of mankind, while Trophonius and Aga-
medes, sons of Erginus, men dear to the immortal
gods, built the approaches of stone.

Thus the divine origin of the temple is vindi-
cated, the structure described, and the human architects honoured, whose descendants, very likely,
were present to hear their ancestors' praise. But
here a puzzling fact challenges the attention and
stimulates the fancy of the poet: Apollo was a
Dorian deity, yet his chief shrine was here upon
Phocian ground. Perhaps some traditions remained to suggest an explanation of the anomaly;
at any rate the poet is not at a loss for an account
of the matter. The temple being established,
Apollo bethought himself what race of priests he

should make its ministers: at least, such is the naïve account in the poem, which expects us to forget that temples do not arise in the absence of predetermined servants and worshippers. While pondering this question, however, Apollo cast his eyes on the sea where it chanced that a swift ship, manned by many and excellent Cretans, was merrily sailing: whereupon the god, taking the form of a huge dolphin, leapt into the ship, to the infinite surprise and bewilderment of those worthy merchants, who, as innocent as the fishers of the Galilæan Lake of the religious destiny that awaited them, were thinking only of the pecuniary profits of their voyage. The presence of the god benumbed their movements, and they stood silent while the ship sailed before the wind. And the blast, veering at this place with the changed configuration of the coast, blew them irresistibly to the very foot of Parnassus, to the little haven of Crissa. There Apollo appeared to them once more, this time running down to the beach to meet them in the form of

> " A stout and lusty fellow,
> His mighty shoulders covered with his mane ;
> Who sped these words upon the wings of sound :
> ' Strangers, who are ye ? and whence sail ye hither
> The watery ways ?   Come ye to traffic justly
> Or recklessly like pirates of the deep
> Rove ye, adventuring your souls, to bring
> Evil on strangers ?   Why thus sit ye grieving,

D

Nor leap on land, nor strike the mast and lay it
In your black ship ?   For so should traders do
When, sated with the labour of the sea,
They quit their painted galley for the shore,
And presently the thought of needful food
Comes gladsomely upon them.'   So he spake,
Putting new courage in their breasts.   To whom
The Cretan captain in his turn replied :
' Since thou art nothing like to things of earth
In form or stature, but most like the gods
That ever live, Hail, and thrice hail, O Stranger,
And may the gods pour blessings on thy head.
Now tell me truly, for I need to know,
What land is this, what people, from what race
Descended ?   As for us, over the deep
Broad sea, we sought another haven, Pylos,
Sailing from Crete, for thence we boast to spring ;
But now our ship is cast upon this shore,
For some god steered our course against our will.'
Then the far-darter spoke and answered them.
' Friends, in well-wooded Cnossus hitherto
Ye have had homes, but ye shall not again
Return to your good native town, to find
Each his fair house and well-belovèd wife,
But here shall ye possess my temple, rich
And greatly honoured by the tribes of men.
For I am son to Zeus.   Apollo is
My sacred name.   'Twas I that led you hither
Over the mighty bosom of the deep,
Intending you no ill ; for ye shall here
Possess a temple sacred to me, rich,
And greatly honoured of all mortal men.
The counsels of the deathless gods shall be
Revealed to you, and by their will your days
Shall pass in honour and in peace for ever.
Come then and, as I bid, make haste to do.
. . .   Build by the sea an altar ; kindle flame ;

Sprinkle white barley grains thereon, and pray,
Standing about the altar. And as first
Ye saw me leap into your swift black bark
In likeness of a dolphin, so henceforth
Worship me by the name Delphinius,
And Delphian ever be my far-seen shrine.' "

Thus the establishment of the Dorian god in
Phocis is explained, and the wealth and dignity
of his temple are justified by prophecy and by
divine intention. For Apollo is not satisfied with
repeatedly describing the future temple, by an incidental epithet, as opulent; that hint would not
have been enough for the simplicity of those mer-
chant sailors, new as they were to the mysteries of
priestcraft. It was necessary for Apollo to allay
their fears of poverty by a more explicit assurance
that it will be easy for them to live by the altar.
And what is more, Hermes and all the thieves he
inspires will respect the shrine; its treasures,
although unprotected by walls, shall be safe for-
ever.

These were truly, as we see, the hymns of a
levitical patriotism. With Homeric breadth and
candour they dilated on the miracles, privileges,
and immunities of the sacred places and their ser-
vitors, and they thus kept alive in successive generations an awe mingled with familiar interest
toward divine persons and things which is characteristic of that more primitive age. Gods and

men were then nearer together, and both yielded more frankly to the tendency, inherent in their nature, to resemble one another.

The same quality is found in another fragment, the most beautiful and the most familiar of all. This is the hymn to Demeter in which two stories are woven together, one telling of the rape of Persephone, and the other of the reception of Demeter, disguised in her sorrow, into the household of Celeus, where she becomes the nurse of his infant son Demophoon. Both stories belong to the religion of Eleusis, where this version of them seems intended to be sung. The place was sacred to Demeter and Persephone and its mysteries dealt particularly with the passage of souls to the nether world and with their habitation there. The pathetic beauty of the first fable — in which we can hardly abstain from seeing some symbolical meaning — expresses for us something of the mystic exaltation of the local rites; while the other tale of Celeus, his wife, his daughters, and his son, whom his nurse, the disguised goddess, almost succeeds in endowing with immortality, celebrates the ancient divine affinities of the chiefs of the Eleusinian state.

The first story is too familiar to need recounting; who has not heard of the gentle Persephone gathering flowers in the meadow and suddenly swallowed by the yawning earth and carried away

to Hades, the god of the nether world, to share
his sombre but sublime dominion over the shades?
— a dignity of which she is not insensible, much
as she grieves at the separation from her beloved
mother; and how Demeter in turn is disconsolate
and (in her wrath and despair at the indifference of the gods) conceals her divinity, refuses
the fruits of the earth, and wanders about in the
guise of an old woman, nursing her grief, until
at last Zeus sends his messenger to Hades to
effect a compromise; and Persephone, after eating
the grain of pomegranate that obliges her to return
yearly to her husband, is allowed to come back to
the upper world to dwell for two-thirds of the year
in her mother's company.

The underlying allegory is here very interesting.
We observe how the genius of the Greek religion,
while too anthropomorphic to retain any clear
consciousness of the cosmic processes that were
symbolized by its deities and their adventures, was
anthropomorphic also in a moral way, and tended
to turn the personages which it ceased to regard
as symbols of natural forces into types of human
experience. So the parable of the seed that must
die if it is to rise again and live an immortal, if
interrupted, life in successive generations, gives
way in the tale of Demeter and Persephone, to
a prototype of human affection. The devotee, no
longer reminded by his religion of any cosmic laws,

was not reduced to a mere superstition, — to a fable and a belief in the efficacy of external rites, — he was encouraged to regard the mystery as the divine counterpart of his own experience. His religion in forgetting to be natural had succeeded in becoming moral; the gods were now models of human endurance and success; their histories offered sublime consolations to mortal destiny. Fancy had turned the aspects of Nature into persons; but devotion, directed upon these imaginary persons, turned them into human ideals and into patron saints, thereby relating them again to life and saving them from insignificance.

A further illustration of the latter transformation may be found in the second story contained in our hymn. Demeter, weary of her wanderings and sick at heart, has come to sit down beside a well, near the house of Celeus. His four young daughters, dancing and laughing, come to fetch water in their golden jars, —

> "As hinds or heifers gambol in the fields
>   When Spring is young."

They speak kindly to the goddess, who asks them for employment. "And for me," she says, —

> "And for me, damsels, harbour pitiful
> And favouring thoughts, dear children, that I come
> To some good man's or woman's house, to ply
> My task in willing service of such sort

As agèd women use.   A tender child
I could nurse well and safely in my arms,
And tend the house, and spread the master's couch
Recessed in the fair chamber, or could teach
The maids their handicraft."

The offer is gladly accepted, for Celeus himself
has an infant son, Demophoon, the hope of his race.
The aged woman enters the dwelling, making in her
long-robed grief a wonderful contrast to the four
sportive girls: —

" Who lifting up their ample kirtle-folds
Sped down the waggon-furrowed way, and shook
Their curls about their shoulders — yellow gold
Like crocuses in bloom."

Once within the house, which she awes with her
uncomprehended presence, the goddess sits absorbed in grief, until she is compelled to smile for
a moment at the jests of the quick-witted maid
Iambe, and consents to take in lieu of the wine that
is offered her, a beverage of beaten barley, water,
and herbs.   These details are of course introduced
to justify the ritual of Eleusis, in which the clown
and the barley-water played a traditional part.

Thus Demeter becomes nurse to Demophoon, but
she has ideas of her duties differing from the common, and worthy of her unusual qualifications. She
neither suckles nor feeds the infant but anoints him
with ambrosia and lays him at night to sleep on the
embers of the hearth. This his watchful mother

discovers with not unnatural alarm; when the goddess reveals herself and departs, foiled in her desire to make her nursling immortal.

The spirit that animates this fable is not that poetic frivolity which we are accustomed to associate with Paganism. Here we find an immortal in profoundest grief and mortals entertaining an angel unawares; we are told of supernatural food, and of a burning fire that might make this mortal put on immortality did not the generous but ignorant impulses of the natural man break in upon that providential purpose and prevent its consummation. Eleusis was the natural home for such a myth, and we may well believe that those initiated into the mysteries there were taught to dwell on its higher interpretation.

But there are other hymns in a lighter vein in which the play of fancy is not guided by any moral intuition. The hymn to Hermes is one perpetual ebullition of irresponsible humour.

Hermes is the child of Maia, a nymph of Cyllene whose cave Zeus has surreptitiously visited while the white-armed Juno — for, unsympathetic prude as this goddess may be, she must still be beautiful —slept soundly in Olympus. The child is hardly born when he catches a tortoise, kills it, scoops out the shell, and makes a lute of it, upon which he begins to play delicious music. Not satisfied with that feat, however, he escapes from his cradle, and drives from their pasture the kine that Apollo has left feeding there. Accused afterward of this mischief, he defends himself after the following fashion, while he lies in his crib, holding his new-made lyre lightly in his hand under the bedclothes. I quote Shelley's version: —

> " ' An ox-stealer should be both tall and strong
>   And I am but a little new-born thing
> Who yet, at least, can think of nothing wrong.
>   My business is to suck, and sleep, and fling
> The cradle-clothes about me all day long,
>   Or, half-asleep, hear my sweet mother sing
> And to be washed in water clean and warm
> And hushed and kissed and kept secure from harm.' "

> *   *   *   *   *   *   *   *

> " Sudden he changed his plan, and with strange skill
>   Subdued the strong Latonian, by the might
> Of winning music, to his mightier will.
>   His left hand held the lyre, and in his right
> The plectrum struck the chords : unconquerable
>   Up from beneath his hand in circling flight
> The gathering music rose — and sweet as Love
> The penetrating notes did live and move

> " Within the heart of great Apollo. He
>   Listened with all his soul, and laughed for pleasure.
> Close to his side stood harping fearlessly
>   The unabashèd boy, and to the measure
> Of the sweet lyre there followed loud and free
>   His joyous voice : for he unlocked the treasure
> Of his deep song, illustrating the birth
> Of the bright Gods, and the dark desert Earth ;

> " And how to the Immortals every one
>   A portion was assigned of all that is.

> But chief Mnemosyne did Maia's son
>   Clothe in the light of his loud melodies.
> And, as each god was born or had begun,
>   He in their order due and fit degrees
> Sung of his birth and being — and did move
> Apollo to unutterable love."

In fact, after the most enthusiastic encomiums
on the young god's art, and on the power of music
in general, Apollo offers the child his protection
and friendship : —

> " Now, since thou hast, although so very small,
>   Science of arts so glorious, thus I swear, —
> And let this cornel javelin, keen and tall,
>   Witness between us what I promise here, —
> That I will lead thee to the Olympian hall,
>   Honoured and mighty, with thy mother dear,
> And many glorious gifts in joy will give thee
> And even at the end will ne'er deceive thee."

Hermes is not insensible to this offer and its advantages; he accepts it with good grace and many
compliments, nor does he wish to remain behind
in the exchange of courtesies and benefits : he addresses Apollo thus : —

> " Thou canst seek out and compass all that wit
>   Can find or teach.   Yet, since thou wilt, come, take
> The lyre — be mine the glory giving it —
>   Strike the sweet chords, and sing aloud, and wake
> The joyous pleasure out of many a fit
>   Of trancèd sound — and with fleet fingers make
> Thy liquid-voicèd comrade speak with thee, —
> It can talk measured music eloquently.

" Then bear it boldly to the revel loud,
   Love-wakening dance, or feast of solemn **state,**
A joy by night or day : for those endowed
   With art and wisdom who interrogate
It teaches, babbling in delightful mood
   All things which make the spirit most elate,
Soothing the mind with sweet familiar play,
Chasing the heavy shadows of dismay.

" To those that are unskilled in its sweet tongue,
   Though they should question most impetuously
Its hidden soul, it gossips something wrong —
   Some senseless and impertinent reply.
But thou, who art as wise as thou art strong,
   Canst compass all that thou desirest.   I
Present thee with this music-flowing shell,
Knowing thou canst interrogate it well. . . ."

Apollo is not slow to learn the new art with
which he is ever after to delight both gods and
men; but he is not at first quite at ease in his
mind, fearing that Hermes will not only recapture
the lyre but steal his friend's bow and arrows into
the bargain.   Hermes, however, swears by all that
is holy never to do so, and the friendship of the
two artful gods is sealed for ever.   The minstrel
does not forget, at this point, to remind his hearers,
among whom we may imagine not a few professional followers of Hermes to have been mixed,
that the robber's honour is pledged by his divine
patron to respect the treasures of Apollo's shrines.
Let not the votary think, he adds, that Apollo's
oracles are equally useful to good and to bad men:

these mysteries are truly efficacious only for the
pious and orthodox who follow the established
traditions of the temple and honour its servants.
Apollo says:—

> "He who comes consigned
> By voice and wings of perfect augury
> To my great shrine shall find avail in me :
>
> "Him I will not deceive, but will assist.
>   But he who comes relying on such birds
>   As chatter vainly, who would strain and twist
>   The purpose of the gods with idle words,
>   And deems their knowledge light, he shall have missed
>   His road — whilst I among my other hoards
> His gifts deposit. . . ."

The wildest fairy-story thus leads easily to a
little drama not without its human charm and moral
inspiration; while the legend is attached to the
cultus, and the cultus is intertwined with the practice and sanctions of daily life. Even here, in its
most playful mood, therefore, this mythological
poetry retains the spirit and function of religion.
Even here sacerdotal interests are not forgotten.
Delphi shall be safe; the lyre is Apollo's by right
although it be Hermes' by invention. A certain
amiable harmony is after all drawn from the riot
of foolishness. All is sweet and unmalicious and
lovable enough, and the patronage of both the
friendly gods, the enthusiast and the wag, may be
invoked with confidence and benefit.

Not less remarkable, although for other reasons,

is the hymn to Aphrodite. Here we find a more human fable and a more serious tone: while the poem, if we choose to consider it in its allegorical meaning, touches one of the deepest convictions of the Greek conscience. All the gods save three — Athena, Artemis, and Hestia, — are subject to the power of Aphrodite, Zeus at least as much as the rest. In revenge for this subjection, Zeus determines to make Aphrodite feel the passion which she boasts to be able to inspire in others.

The fair shepherd Anchises feeds his flocks upon Mount Ida, and with him Aphrodite is made to fall in love. She presents herself to him in a human disguise, and meets his advances with a long account of her birth and parentage, and begs him to take her back to her parents, and having asked for her hand and fulfilled all customary formalities, to lead her away as his lawful wife. The passion which at the same time, however, she is careful to breathe into him cannot brook so long a delay : and she yields to his impatience. When about to leave him she awakes him from his sleep, turns upon him the full glance of her divinity, and reveals her name and his destiny. She will bear him a son, Æneas, who will be one of the greatest princes and heroes of Troy ; but he himself will be stricken with feebleness and a premature old age, in punishment for the involuntary sacrilege which he has committed.

The description of the disguised goddess, with
its Homeric pomp and elaborate propriety, is a
noble and masterly one, underlined, as it were,
with a certain satirical or dramatic intention; we
have the directness of a Nausicaa, with a more
luxurious and passionate beauty. The revelation
of the goddess is wonderfully made, with that
parallel movement of natural causes and divine
workings which is so often to be admired in
Homer. The divinity of the visitant appears only
at the moment of her flight, when she becomes a
consecration and an unattainable memory. The
sight of deity leaves the eyes dull, like those of
the Platonic prisoners returning from the sunlight
of truth into the den of appearance. Nay more,
a communion with the divinity, closer than is
consonant with human frailty, leaves the seer impotent and a burden upon the world; but this
personal tragedy is not without its noble fruits to
posterity. Anchises suffers, but his son Æneas,
the issue of that divine though punishable union,
lives to bear, not only the aged Anchises himself,
but the gods of Ilium, out of the ruins of Troy.

Such analogies carry us, no doubt, far beyond
the intention of the hymn or of the exoteric religion to which it ministers. The story-teller's
delight in his story is the obvious motive of such
compositions, even when they reflect indirectly
the awe in which the divine impersonations of

natural forces were held by the popular religion. All that we may fairly imagine to have been in the mind of the pious singer is the sense that something divine comes down among us in the crises of our existence, and that this visitation is fraught with immense although vague possibilities of both good and evil. The gods sometimes appear, and when they do they bring us a foretaste of that sublime victory of mind over matter which we may never gain in experience but which may constantly be gained in thought. When natural phenomena are conceived as the manifestation of divine life, human life itself, by sympathy with that ideal projection of itself, enlarges its customary bounds, until it seems capable of becoming the life of the universe. A god is a conceived victory of mind over Nature. A visible god is the consciousness of such a victory momentarily attained. The vision soon vanishes, the sense of omnipotence is soon dispelled by recurring conflicts with hostile forces; but the momentary illusion of that realized good has left us with the perennial knowledge of good as an ideal. Therein lies the essence and the function of religion.

That such a function was fulfilled by this Homeric legend, with all its love of myth and lust of visible beauty, is witnessed by another short hymn, which we may quote almost entire by way of conclusion. It is addressed to Castor and Poly-

deuces, patrons of sailors no less than of horsemen
and boxers.   It is impossible to read it without
feeling that the poet, however entangled he may
have been in superstition and fable, grasped that
high essence of religion which makes religion
rational.   He felt the power of contemplation
to master the contradictions of life and to over-
spread experience, sublime but impalpable, like a
rainbow over retreating storms : —

> ' Ye wild-eyed Muses, sing the Twins of Jove
> . . . Mild Pollux, void of blame,
> And steed-subduing Castor, heirs of fame.
> These are the powers who earth-born mortals save
> And ships, whose flight is swift along the wave.
> When wintry tempests o'er the savage sea
> Are raging, and the sailors tremblingly
> Call on the Twins of Jove with prayer and vow,
> Gathered in fear upon the lofty prow,
> And sacrifice with snow-white lambs — the wind
> And the huge billow bursting close behind
> Even then beneath the weltering waters bear
> The staggering ship, — they suddenly appear,
> On yellow wings rushing athwart the sky,
> And lull the blasts in mute tranquillity
> And strew the waves on the white ocean's bed,
> Fair omen of the voyage ; from toil and dread
> The sailors rest, rejoicing in the sight,
> And plough the quiet sea in safe delight." [1]

[1] Shelley's translation.

III

THE DISSOLUTION OF PAGANISM

GREEK religion seems to have contained three factors of unequal prominence, but ultimately of about equal importance and longevity. Most obvious, especially if we begin our study with Homer, is the mythology which presents us with a multitude of gods, male and female, often related by blood, and having social and even hostile relations with one another. If we examine their characters, attributes, and fables, we readily perceive that most of them are impersonations of natural forces. Some, however, figure prominently as patrons of special arts or special places, as Apollo of prophecy and music, of Delos and Delphi; and yet others seem to be wholly personifications of human powers, as Athena of prudence and of martial and industrial arts.

Underlying this mythology is another element, probably more ancient, the worship of ancestors, local divinities, and domestic gods. With these were naturally connected various ritual observances, and especially the noblest and most impor-

E

49

tant of rites, the sacrifice. Such practices may be
supposed to have belonged originally to the tribal
religion, and to have passed by analogy to the great
natural gods, when these had been once created by
the poet and perhaps identified with the older
genius of that spot where their efficacy was first
signally manifested.

Finally, as a third element, we find the religion
of the priests, soothsayers, and magicians, as well as
the rites of Orpheus, Bacchus, and the Great
Goddesses at Eleusis. These forms of worship
showed Oriental affinities and partook of a kind of
nocturnal horror and mystical enthusiasm. They
were the Greek representatives of the religion of
revelation and of sacraments, and bore much the
same relation to the supernaturalistic elements in
Christianity as does the idea of a shade in Hades
to the idea of a soul in heaven. The fundamental
intuitions were the same, but in Pagan times they
remained vague, doubtful, and incoherent.

These three forms of religion lay together in
men's minds and habits throughout the formative
period of Greek literature. There was an occasional rivalry among them, but the tolerance characteristic of Paganism could reconcile their claims
without much difficulty, and admit them all to
a share of honour. The history of the three
elements, however, differs essentially, as might be
expected after a consideration of their respective

natures. The antique family religion lived by inertia; it was obeyed without being justified theoretically, and remained strong by its very obscurity. Many customs which a man may have occasion to conform to only once or twice in his life endure for ages and survive the ebb and flow of intellectual and political systems. Nursery tales, trivial superstitions, customs connected with weddings or funerals, or with certain days of the year, have a strange and irrational persistence; they surprise us by emerging into prominence after centuries of a sort of subterraneous existence. Thus the deification of Roman emperors was not the sacrilegious innovation which it might appear to be, but on the contrary a restoration of the spirit of the most ancient faith, a revival called to the aid of a new polity by the mingled statecraft and superstition of the times. Thus, too, the Christian care in the burial of the dead (contrary as it is to the theoretical spiritualism of Christianity), the feast of All Souls, and the prayers for the departed are evidences of the same latent human religion underlying the cosmic flights and public controversies of theology.

The mysteries, on the other hand, had essentially a spirit of self-consciousness and propaganda. They came as revelations or as reforms; they pretended to disclose secrets handed down from remote antiquity, from the primeval revelation of God to

man, or truths recovered by the inspiration of
later prophets supernaturally illumined.   The
history of these movements is, accordingly, the
history of sects.   They never constituted the normal and common religion of the people, and never
impressed their spirit on the national literature.
Æschylus or Plato may have borrowed something
from them; but they did so most when they
assumed an attitude of open opposition to the
exoteric religion of their country.   Thus when
Plato makes his Socrates propound a Pythagorean
or Orphic doctrine of transmigration, he represents
the very members of the Socratic circle as surprised,
or as incredulous; and when they are finally
silenced by the proofs advanced, it is only because
they are overawed by the dogmatic unction of a
dying sage, who stimulates their imagination with
poetic myths, and confuses their intellect with
verbal equivocations.   When the mist of the argument has cleared away, like incense after the
sacrifice, there remains indeed a profound emotion,
a catharsis produced by the sublimity and pathos,
so artfully mingled, of both scene and argument;
but the bare doctrine enunciated, true and profound
as it is in its deeper meaning, is quite incapable of
appealing to an undisciplined mind, and could not
pass for a religious dogma except for the priestly
robes in which it is dressed.   Thus the function of
the mysteries of which Plato's Phædo may be

regarded as a philosophic echo, was to be the vehicle of revolutionary tendencies, tendencies which a philosopher might privately shape in one way and a superstitious man in another. Both could find in the spell of an occult ceremonial and in the prophecies of an oracular creed an escape from the limitations of the official religion. Mysticism and the claim to illumination found in these mysteries their natural expression. The many fundamental questions left unanswered and unasked by Paganism, the many potentialities of religious emotion left unexercised by it, were thus allowed to appear.

Independently of these two comparatively silent streams of religious life, we may trace the current of polytheistic theology, — a current which naturally left a plainer trace in literature, since it contained all there might be in Greece of speculation and controversy in religious matters. The moral sanctions of religion were embodied in the domestic and civic worship; the pious imagination remained thereby all the freer to follow the analogies of physical objects in its mythology. Apollo was the father of Asclepius and the leader of the Muses; his ideal dignity and beneficence were vouched for by those attributes. He could well afford, therefore, as the Sun-god, to decimate the Greek army with the same fatal shafts with which he slew the Python. The moral function of the god was certain on other grounds, being enshrined in the local religions of the people. The poet might follow without scruple the suggestions of experience; he might attribute to the god the various activities, beneficent and maleficent, observable in the element over which he presided. This is a liberty taken even in the most moralistic religions. In the Gospels, for instance, we sometimes find the kingdom of heaven illustrated by principles drawn from observation of this world rather than from an ideal conception of justice; as when we hear that to him that hath shall be given and from him that hath not shall be taken away even that which he hath. Such characterizations appeal to our sense of fact. They remind us that the God we are seeking is present and active, that he is the living God; they are doubtless necessary if we are to keep religion from passing into a mere idealism and God into the vanishing point of our thought and endeavour. For we naturally seek to express his awful actuality, his unchallengeable power, no less than his holiness and beauty. This sense of the real existence of religious objects can only be maintained by identifying them with objects of actual experience, with the forces of Nature, or the passions or conscience of man, or (if it must come to that) with written laws or visible images.

An instinctive recognition of this necessity kept Greek mythology ever ready to return to Nature to gather its materials afresh from a docile, if poetical, observation of reality. The character of the god must be studied in the manifestations of his chosen element; otherwise men might forget that, although the form of the god was poetical, his essence was a positive reality of the most practical kind. Zeus must still toss his ambrosial locks with a certain irritation, in order that we may recognize him in the rumblings of the sky; he must still be capable of wrath and deliberate malice, that his awful hand may be thought to have hurled the thunderbolt. Cronos must not be forbidden to devour his children, else we should no longer reverence in him the inexorable might of time. Mythology was quite right in not shrinking from such poetic audacities. They were its chief title to legitimacy, the proof, amid the embroideries of fancy which overlay the divine idea, that the god was not an invention, but a fact. He had been found, he was known. His character, like all character, was merely a principle which reflection discovered in his observed conduct. The reality, then, of the mythological gods was initially unquestionable; and the more faithful the study of Nature by which the poet was inspired, the more authority did his prophetic vision retain.

But the intense imaginative vitality that must have preceded Homer and Hesiod, the prodigious gift of sympathetic observation to which we owe

Zeus and Pan and all their endless retinue, was too
glorious to last. No later interpreter could find so
much meaning in his text. Mythology was accordingly placed in a sad dilemma, with either horn
fatal to its life; it must either be impoverished to
remain sincere, or become artificial to remain adequate. The history of Greek religion, on its speculative side, is nothing but the story of this double
decadence. Reflection upon the process of Nature
and desire for philosophic truth led inevitably to
a blank pantheism and to the reduction of positive
traditions to moral allegories. This was the direction taken by the Stoic theology. On the other
hand, adherence to the traditional gods, with no
further vivifying reference to their natural functions in the world, could lead only to arbitrary
fictions, which, having no foothold or justification
in reality, were incapable of withstanding the first
sceptical attack. What an age of imagination had
intuited as truth, an age of reflection could preserve
only as fable; and as fable, accordingly, the religion
of the ancients survived throughout the Christian
ages. It remains still the mother-tongue of the
imagination and, in spite of all revolutions and
admixtures, is the classic language of art and
poetry, which no other means of expression has
superseded.

Beginning, however, with that zealous Protestant,
the old Xenophanes, the austerer minds, moralists,

naturalists, and wits, united in decrying the fanciful polytheism of the poets. This criticism was in
one sense unjust; it did not consider the original
justification of mythology in human nature and in
the external facts. It was, like all heresy or partial
scepticism, in a sense superficial and unphilosophi-
cal. It was far from conceiving that its own tenets
and assumptions were as groundless, without being
as natural or adequate, as the system it attacked.
To a person sufficiently removed by time or by
philosophy from the controversies of sects, orthodoxy must always appear right and heresy wrong;
for he sees in orthodoxy the product of the creative
mind, of faith and constructive logic, but in heresy
only the rebellion of some partial interest or partial
insight against the corollaries of a formative principle imperfectly grasped and obeyed with hesita-
tion. At a distance, the criticism that disintegrates
any great product of art or mind must always appear
short-sighted and unamiable. Socrates, invoking
the local deities of brooks and meadows, or paying
the debt of a cock to Asclepius (in thanksgiving,
it is said, for a happy death), is more reasonable
and noble to our mind than are the hard denials of
Xenophanes or Theodorus. But in their day the
revolt of the sceptics had its relative justification.
The imagination had dried up, and what had once
been a natural interpretation of facts now seemed an
artificial addition to them. An elaborate and irrel-

evant world of fiction seemed to have been imposed on human credulity. Mythology was, in
fact, already largely irrelevant; the experience
poetized by it had been forgotten and the symbol,
in its insignificance, could not be honestly or use-
fully retained.

The Greek philosophers, as a rule, proceeded
cautiously in these matters. They passed mythology by with a conventional reverence and looked
elsewhere for the true object of their personal
religion. But the old mythological impulse was
not yet spent; it showed itself still active in all
the early philosophers who gave the godhead new
incarnations congruous with the character of their
respective physical systems. To the Socratic
School the natural world was no longer the sphere
in which divinity was to be found. They looked
for the divine rather in moral and intelligible
ideas. But not only did they carry the mythological instinct with them into that new field, they
also retained it in the field of Nature, whenever
they still regarded Nature as real. Thus Aristotle,
while he rejected the anthropomorphism of the
popular faith, attributing it to political exigencies,
turned the forty-nine spheres, of which he con-
jectured that the heaven might be composed, into
a pantheon of forty-nine divinities. Every primary movement, he argued, must be the expression
of an eternal essence by which the movement is

justified, as the movement of the mind in thinking
or loving is justified by the truth or excellence of
the object of thought or of love.   Without such a
worthy object, these spiritual activities would be
irrational; and no less irrational would be the
motion of the spheres, were each not obedient to
the influence of some sacred and immutable principle.   Forty-nine gods accordingly exist; but no
more.   For, since the essence of each is to be the
governing ideal of a motion, the number of motions
in the sky determines the number of divine first
principles.   The gods, we see, are still the souls
of Nature; a soul without a body would be a
principle without an application; there can be
no gods, then, without a phenomenal function,
no gods that do not appear in the operations of
Nature.   This astronomic mythology was surely
not less poetical than that of Homer, even if, by
virtue of a certain cold and abstract purity, not
unworthy of the stars of which it spoke, it was
more difficult and sublime.   We may observe in
it a last application of the ancient mythological
method by which the phenomena of Nature became
evidence of the existence and character of the
gods.

But the celestial deities of Aristotle, and the
minor creative gods of Plato that correspond to
them, retained too much poetic individuality for the
still poorer imagination of later times.   The most

religious of sects during the classical decadence was that of the Stoics; in them the spirit of conformity, which is a chief part even of the religions of hope, constituted by its exclusive cultivation a religion of despair. The name of Zeus, and an equally equivocal use of the word "reason" to designate the regularity of Nature, served to disguise the alien brutality of the power or law to which all the gods had been reduced. Against the background of a materialistic pantheism, in which Stoic speculation culminated, two positive interests stood out: one, the resolute and truly human courage with which the Stoic faced the reality as he conceived it, and kept his dignity and his conscience pure although heaven might fall; the other, the efforts he made, in his need for religion, to rejuvenate and reinterpret the pagan forms. The fables he turned into ethical allegories, the oracles, auspices, and other superstitious rites, he transformed into quasi-scientific ways of reading the book of Nature and forecasting events.

This possibility of prophecy constituted the Stoic "providence" which the sentimentality of modern apologists has been glad to confuse with the *benevolent* Providence of Christian dogma, a Providence making for the salvation of men. The Stoic providence excluded that essential element of benevolence; it was merely the fact that Nature was prophetic of her own future, that her parts, both in space and in time, were magically composed into one living system. Mythology thus ended with the conception of a single god whose body was the whole physical universe, whose fable was all history, and whose character was the principle of the universal natural order. No attempt was made by the ancient Stoics to make this divinity better or more amiable than the evidence of experience showed it to be; the self-centred, self-sufficient Stoic morality, the recourse to suicide, and the equality in happiness and dignity between the wise man and Zeus, all prove quite conclusively that nothing more was asked or expected of Nature than what she chose to give; to be virtuous was in man's power, and nothing else was a good to man. The universe could neither benefit nor injure him; and thus we see that, despite a reverential tone and an occasional reminiscence of the thunderbolts of Zeus, the Stoic's conscience knew how to scorn the moral nothingness of that blank deity to which his metaphysics had reduced the genial company of the gods.

Thus the reality which the naturalistic gods had borrowed from the elements proved to be a dangerous prerogative; being real and manifest, these gods had to be conceived according to our experience of their operation, so that with every advance in scientific observation theology had to be revised, and something had to be subtracted from the person-

ality and benevolence of the gods.   The moral
character originally attributed to them necessarily
receded before the clearer definition of natural
forces and the accumulated experience of national
disasters.   Finally, little remained of the gods
except their names, reduced to rhetorical synonyms
for the various departments of Nature; Phœbus
was nothing but a bombastic way of saying the
sun; Hephæstus became nothing but fire, Eros or
Aphrodite nothing but love, Zeus nothing but the
general force and law of Nature.   Thus the gods
remained real, but were no longer gods.   If belief
in their reality was to be kept up, they could not
retain too many attributes that had no empirical
manifestation.   They must be reduced, as it were,
to their fighting weight.   All that the imagination
had added to them by way of personal character,
sanctity, and life must be rejected as anthropomorphism and fable.

Such is the necessary logic of natural religion.
If Nature manifests the existence of a god, she
must to that extent manifest his character; if she
does not manifest his character, she cannot involve
his existence.   We observe to-day a process exactly
analogous to that by which the natural divinities
of Greece were reduced again to the physical or
social forces from which poetry had originally
evoked their forms.   Many minds are grown too
timid to build their religious faith unblushingly on

revelation, or on that moral imagination or inward demand which revelation comes to express and to satisfy. They seek, therefore, to naturalize the Deity and to identify it with some principle of history, of Nature, or of logic. But this identification cannot be made without great concessions on both sides. The accommodations which ensue inevitably involve many equivocations, and some misrepresentations of the heterogeneous principles, now natural, now moral, which it is sought to unify. Confused and agonized by these contradictions, the natural theologian, if he keep his honesty, can only rest in the end in a chastened recognition of the facts of experience, toward which he will, no doubt, exercise his acquired habits of acquiescence and euphemism. But these habits, the survival of which gives his philosophy some air of being still a religion, will not be inherited by his disciples and successors; a pious manner may survive religious faith, but will not survive it long. The society to whom the reformer teaches a reticent and embarrassed naturalism will discard the reticence and avow the naturalism with pride. The masses of men will see no reason why they should not live out their native impulses or acquired passions without fear of that environing power of which they are, after all, the highest embodiment; while a few thinkers, devout and rational by temperament, will know how to main-

tain their dignity of spirit in the face of a universe
of which they ask no favour save the revelation of
its laws. Thus irreligion for the many and Stoicism
for the few is the end of natural religion in the
modern world as it was in the ancient.

But natural religion (that is, the turning of the
facts and laws of Nature or of experience into an
object of worship) is by no means a primitive nor an
ultimate form of religion; it is rather of all the
forms of religion the most unnatural and the least
capable of existing without a historical and emotional setting, independent of its own essence and
inconsistent with its principle.   No nation has ever
had a merely natural religion. What is called by
that name has been the appanage of a few philosophers in ages of religious disintegration, when the
habit of worship, surviving the belief in any proper
object of worship, has been transferred with effort
and uncertainty to the natural order which alone
remained before the mind, — to the cosmos, the
self, the state, or humanity. Mythology, of which
natural religion is the last and most abstract phase,
was originally religious only in so far as it was
supernatural; in so far, I mean, as the analogies of
outer Nature led the poet to conceive some moral
ideal, some glorious being full of youth and serenity,
of passion and wisdom. Only when thus transfigured into the human could the natural seem
divine. The Greeks were never idolaters, and no

more worshipped the sun or moon or the whole of Nature than they did statues of bronze or marble; they worshipped only the god who had a temporal image in the temple as he had an eternal image in the sun or in the universe.

It happened, therefore, that in the decay of mythology the gods could still survive as moral ideals. The more they were cut off from their accidental foothold in the world of fact, the more clearly could they manifest their essence as expressions of the world of values. We have mentioned the fact that the greater gods of Greece were almost wholly detached from the cosmographical hints which had originally suggested their character and fable. Thus emancipated, these nobler gods could survive in the consciousness of the devout, fixed there by their purely moral significance and poetic truth. Apollo or Athena showed little or nothing of a naturalistic origin; they were patrons of life, embodiments of the ideal, objects of contemplation for souls that by prayer would rise to the semblance of the god to whom they prayed. This transformation into the moral had been going on from the beginning in the religious mind of Greece. It was really the legitimate fulfilment of that translation into the human to which mythology itself was due. But mythology had merely turned the physical into the personal and impassioned; religion was now to turn the psychical into the

F

good. This tendency came to a vivid and rational expression in Plato. The gods, he declared, should be represented only as they were, *i.e.* as moral ideals. The scandal of their fables should be removed and they should be regarded as authors only of the good, in their own lives as in ours. To refer all things to the efficacy of the gods should be accounted impiety. They, like the supreme and abstract principle of all excellence which they embodied, could be the authors only of what is good.

Had this remarkable doctrine been carried out fully it would have led to important results. We should have had goodness as the criterion of divinity, to the exclusion of power. God would have become avowedly an ideal, a pattern to which the world might or might not conform. Such potential conformity would have remained dependent on causes, natural or free, with which God, not being a power, could have nothing to do. Plato and Aristotle did, in fact, construct a theology on these lines, but they obscured its purity in their wellmeant attempts to connect (more or less mythically or magically) their own Socratic principle of excellence with the cosmic principles of the earlier philosophers. The elements of confusion and pantheism which were thus introduced into the Socratic philosophy made it more acceptable, perhaps, to the theologians of later times, in whose religion a pantheistic tendency was also latent. In the hands of Jewish, Christian, or Mohammedan commentators the mythical and magical part of the Greek conceptions was naturally emphasized and the rational part reinterpreted and obscured. Plato had spoken, in one of his myths, of a Demiurgos, a personification of the Idea of the Good, who directly or indirectly made the world in his own image, rendering it as perfect as the indeterminate Chaos he worked on would allow. Aristotle had spoken of an intelligence, happy and self-contemplative, who was the principle of movement in the heavens, and through the heavens in the rest of Nature. Such expressions had a sound far too congruous with Mosaic doctrine not to be seized upon with joy by the apologists of the new faiths, who were glad to invoke the authority of classic poets and philosophers in favour of doctrines that in their Hebrew expression might so easily seem crude and irrational to the Gentiles. This assimilation gave to the casual myths of Plato and to the meagre though bold argumentation of Aristotle a turn and a significance which they hardly had to their authors. If we approach these philosophers as we should from the point of view of Greek literature and life, and prepare ourselves to see in them the disciples of Socrates rather than (what Plato was once actually declared to be) the disciples of Moses, we shall see that they were simply mythologists of the Ideal; they refined the gods of tradition into patrons of civic discipline and art, the gods of natural philosophy into principles of intelligibility and beauty.

The creation described in the Timæus is a transparent parable. Elements which ethical reflection distinguishes in the field of experience are turned in that dialogue, with undisguised freedom of fancy, into so many half-personified primitive powers; the Ideas, the Demiurgos, Chaos, the Indeterminate, and the "gods of gods." Plato has not forgotten the lessons of Socrates and Parmenides. He distrusts as much as they any natural or genetic philosophy of existence. He virtually tells us that, if we must have a history of creation, we can hardly do better than to take ideal or moral principles, combine them as we might so many material elements, and see how the intelligible part of existence may thus receive a quasi-explanation. God remains the creator of the good only, because what he is mythically said to create is merely that in Nature which spontaneously resembles him or conforms to his idea; only this element in Nature is intelligible or good, and therefore the principle of goodness may be said to be its cause. Thus, for example, if we chose to write an Anatomy of Melancholy, we might attribute to the Demon of Spleen or to the Blue Devils only the sombre elements of that soulful compound, which, however, the evil imps would

eternally tend to make as absolutely dyspeptic
and like unto themselves as its primordial texture
would allow. In exactly such a way Plato, in his
allegorical manner, constructed a universe with a
poetical machinery of moral forces, personified and
treated as agents. When the thin veil of allegory
is drawn aside, there remains nothing but a splendid illustration of the Socratic philosophy; we are
taught that the only science is moral science, and
that, if we wish to understand the world, we must
bend our minds to the definition of its qualities
and values, which are all that is intelligible in it.
Essences and values alone are knowable and fixed
and amenable to science. If we insist on history
and cosmogony, we must be satisfied with having them presented to us in allegorical form, and
made to follow ethics as the Timæus follows the
Republic. Natural philosophy can be nothing
but a sort of analytic retrospect by which we trace
the first glimmerings and the progressive manifestation in Nature of those ideas which have authority
over our own minds.

Phenomena had for Plato existence without
reality, that is, without intelligibility or value.
They were a mere appearance. We need not be
surprised, then, that he refused altogether to construct a theology by the poetic interpretation of
phenomena and preferred to construct one allegori-
cally out of his moral conceptions, the good and the

ideal.   Aristotle, too, while adhering incidentally,
as we have seen, to a purified astronomical theology, capped this with a purified moral theology
of his own.   The Platonic picture-gallery of ideas,
with the abstract principle of excellence that
unified them, gave place in his philosophy to an
Ideal realized in the concrete and existing as an
individual.   We may venture to say that among
the thinkers of all nations Aristotle was the first
to reach the conception of what may fitly be called
God.   Neither the national deity of the Hebrews,
as then conceived, nor the natural deities of the
Gentiles, nor the half-physical, half-logical abstractions of the earlier Greek philosophers really
corresponded to the notion of a being spiritual,
personal, and perfect, immutable without being
abstract, and omnipotent without effort and without degradation.   Aristotle first constructed this
ideal, not out of his fancy, but by building on the
solid ground of human nature and following to
their point of union the lines which moral aspiration and effort actually follow.   Nay, the ideal
he pointed to was to be the goal not of human life
only but of natural life in all its forms.   The
analytic study of Nature (a study which at the
same time must be imaginative and sympathetic)
could guide us to the conception of her inner
needs and tendencies and of what their proper
fulfilment would be.   We could then see that this

fulfilment would lie in intelligence and thought. Growth is for the sake of the fruition of life, and the fruition of life consists in the pursuit and attainment of objects. The moral virtues belong to the pursuit, the intellectual to the attainment. Knowledge is the end of all endeavour, the justification and fulfilment of all growth. Intelligence is the clarification of love.

A being, then, whose life should be a life of pure and complete knowledge, would embody the goal toward which all Nature strives. When we ponder duly the short phrases in which Aristotle propounds his conception of God we find that he has called up before us the noblest possible object of human thought, the presentiment of that thought's perfect fulfilment. There is no alloy of naturalism in this conception, and at the same time no suspicion of irrelevancy. This God is not a mere title of honour for the psycho-physical universe, confusedly conceived and lumped together; he is an ultra-mundane ideal, to be an inviolate standard and goal for all moving reality. Yet he is not irrelevant to the facts and forces of the world, not the dream of an abstracted poet. He is an idea which reality everywhere evokes in evoking its own deepest craving and need. Nothing is so pertinent and momentous in life as the object we are trying to attain by thought or action, since that object is the source of our inspiration and the standard of our success. Thus Aristotle's God is not superfluous, not invented. This theology is a true idealism, I mean an idealism itself purely ideal, which establishes the authority of human demands, ethical, and logical, without impugning the existence or efficacy of that material universe which it endows with a meaning and a standard.

Yet this rational conception, the natural outgrowth of the Socratic philosophy, establishes a dualism between the actual and the ideal against which the human mind easily rebels. Aristotle himself was hardly faithful to it. He tried to prove the existence of his God, and existence is something quite irrelevant to an ideal. This confusion is very excusable, especially in an age when the strictly mechanical view of Nature still seemed hopelessly inadequate. Aristotle consequently tried to understand the natural world by viewing it systematically from the point of view of moral science, as Plato had done less coherently in his myths; and hence came what we must regard as the great error of Aristotle's philosophy, the belief in the efficacy of final causes and in the preëxistence of entelechies. But, apart from this unhappy question of existence, which is, as we have said, irrelevant to an ideal, Aristotle's conception of God remains, perhaps, the most philosophical that has yet been constructed. Without any concessions to sentiment or superstition, it presents us with a sublime vision of the essentially human, of a nature as free from an unworthy anthropomorphism as from an inhuman abstractness. It is made both human and superhuman by the same principle of idealization. It is the final cause of Nature and man, the realization of their imminent upward effort, the essence that would contain all their values and escape all their imperfections.

We may well doubt, however, whether men in general will ever be ready to accept so austere a theology in guise of a religion; they were certainly not ready to do so at the end of the classical period. The inheritance of Paganism fell instead to Christianity, in which ethical and naturalistic elements were again united, although united in a new way. For, while the scheme of Paganism, and of all the philosophies that sought to rationalize Paganism, was cosmic and static, the scheme of Christianity was historical. They spoke of the dynamic relations of heaven and earth, or of the immutable hierarchy of ideas and essences; even Aristotle's God was somehow in spatial relations to the Universe which he set in motion. The religion of the Hebrews, on the other hand, had been essentially historical and civic: it had been concerned with the moral destinies of Israel and the dealings of Jehovah with his people. Christianity inherited this historical character; its mysteries

occurred in time. Not only the redemption of the
world but the vocation and sanctification of the individual were progressive, and when the habits and
problems of Christian theology were carried over
by the German idealists into the region of pure
metaphysics, the systems they conceived were still
systems of evolution. God was to be manifest in
the development of things. For Christianity in its
own way had spoken from the beginning of a gradual and yet to be completed descent of the divine
into the natural by the agency of prophecy, law,
and sacramental institutions; it had represented
the relations of God to man in a vast historic
drama, of which creation constituted the opening,
the fall and redemption the nexus, and the last
judgment the unravelling.

Thus appeared a new scheme for the unification
of the natural and the moral. The harmony which
the old religion had failed to establish in space and
in Nature, the new sought to establish in history
and in time. It was hoped that life and experience, sin and redemption, might manifest that
divinity which had fled out of the sea and sky, and
which it seemed sacrilege to identify any longer
with the animal vitality of the universe. Whether
the same criticism that disintegrated mythology
and isolated its elements of science and of poetry
would not be fatal to the new combination of the
moral and the factual in the history of man, is

hardly a question for us here. Suffice it to point out the problem and to register the solution which was found in the ancient world to the analogous problem that presented itself there. The first impulse of the imagination is always to combine in the object all the elements which lie together in the mind, to project them indiscriminately into a single conception of reality, enriched with as many qualities as there are phases and values in our experience. But these phases and values have diverse origins and do not permanently hang together. It becomes after a while impossible to keep them attached to a single image; they have to be distributed according to their true order and connections, some objectified into a physical universe of mechanism and law, others built into a system of rational objects, into a hierarchy of logical and moral ideas. So the lovely pantheon of the Greeks yielded in time to analysis and was dissolved into abstract science and conscious fable. So, too, the body and soul of later religions may come to be divided, when they render back to earth what they contain of positive history and to the heaven of man's indomitable idealism what they contain of aspiration and hope.

IV

THE POETRY OF CHRISTIAN DOGMA

THE deathbed of Paganism was surrounded by doctors. Some, the Stoics, advised a conversion into pantheism (with an allegorical interpretation of mythology to serve the purposes of edification); others, the Neo-Platonists, prescribed instead a supernatural philosophy, where the efficacy of all traditional rites would be justified by incorporation into a system of universal magic, and the gods would find their place among the legions of spirits and demons that were to people the concentric spheres. But these doctors had no knowledge of the patient's natural constitution; their medicines, prescribed with the best intentions, were in truth poisons and only hastened the inevitable end. Nor had the unfortunate doctors the consolation of being heirs. Parasites that they were, they perished with the patron on whose substance they had fed, and Christianity, their despised rival, came into sole possession.

Yet Neo-Platonism, for all we can see, responded as well as Christianity to the needs of the time,

and had besides great external advantages in its
alliance with tradition, with civil power, and with
philosophy. If the demands of the age were for
a revealed religion and an ascetic morality, Neo-
Platonism could satisfy them to the full. Why,
then, should the Hellenic world have broken with
the creations of its own genius, so plastic, eloquent, and full of resource, to run after foreign
gods and new doctrines that must naturally have
been stumbling-blocks to its prejudices, and foolishness to its intelligence? Shall we say that the
triumph of Christianity was a miracle? Is it not
a doubtful encomium on a religion to say that only
by miracle could it come to be believed? Perhaps the forces of human reason and emotion suffice to explain this faith. We prefer to think so;
otherwise, however complete and final the triumph
of Christianity might be, it would not be justified
or beneficent.

Neo-Platonism arose in the midst of the same
conditions as Christianity. There was weariness
and disgust with the life of nature, decay of political virtue, desire for some personal and supernatural good. It was hardly necessary to preach
the doctrine of original sin to that society; the visible blight that had fallen on classic civilization
was proof enough of that. What it was necessary
to preach was redemption. It was necessary to
point to some sphere of refuge and of healthful

resort, where the ignominies and the frivolities of
this world might be forgotten, and where the hunger of a heart left empty by its corroding passions
might be finally satisfied. But where find such a
supernatural world? By what revelation learn its
nature and be assured of its existence?

Neo-Platonism opened vistas into the supernatural, but the avenues of approach which it had
chosen and the principle which had given form to
its system foredoomed it to failure as a religion.
This avenue was dialectic, and this principle the
hypostasis of abstractions. Plato had pointed out
this path in his genial allegories. He had, by a
poetical figure, turned the ideas of reason into the
component forces of creation. This was, with him,
a method of expression, but being the only method
he was inclined to employ, it naturally entangled
and occasionally, perhaps, deceived his intelligence;
for a poet easily mistakes his inspired tropes for
the physiology of Nature. Yet Platonic dogma,
even when meant as such, retained the transparency
and significance of a myth; philosophy was still a
language for the expression of experience, and dialectic a method and not a creed. But the master's
counters, current during six centuries of intellectual decadence, had become his disciples' money.
Each of his abstractions seemed to them a discovery, each of his metaphors a revelation. The
myths of the great dialogues, and, above all, the

fanciful machinery of the Timæus, interpreted with
an incredible literalness and naïve earnestness, such
as only Biblical exegesis can rival, formed the
starting point of the new revelation. The method
and insight thus obtained were then employed in
filling the *lacunæ* of the system and spreading its
wings wider and wider, until a prodigious hierarchy of supernatural existences had been invented,
from which the natural world was made to depend
as a last link and lowest emanation.

The baselessness and elaboration of this theology
were, of course, far from being obstacles to its success in such an age. On the contrary, the less evidence could be found in common experience for
what a man appeared to know, the more deeply,
people inferred, must he be versed in supernatural
lore, and the greater, accordingly, was his authority. Nor was the spell of personal genius and even
holiness wanting in the leaders of the new philosophy to lend it colour and persuasiveness with the
many, to whom metaphysical conceptions are less
impressive than is an eloquent personality, or a
reputation for miraculous powers. Plotinus, to
speak only of the greatest of the sect, had, in fact,
a notable success in his day. His lectures at Rome,
we are told, were attended by all the fashion and
intellect of the capital; and his large and systematic thought, his subtlety and precision, his comparatively sober eloquence, and his assurance, if we

may say so, in treading the clouds, have made him at all times a great authority with those persons who look in philosophy rather for impressive results than for solid foundations. His contemporaries were eminently persons of that type. A hungry man, when you bring him bread, does not stop to make scrupulous inquiries about the mill or the oven from which you bring it.

But the trouble was that the bread of Plotinus was a stone. The heart cannot feed on thin and elaborate abstractions, irrelevant to its needs and divorced from the natural objects of its interest. Men will often accept the baldest fictions as truths; but it is impossible for them to give a human meaning to vacuous conceptions, or to grow to love the categories of logic, interweaving their image with the actions and emotions of daily life. Religion must spring from the people; it must draw its form from tradition and its substance from the national imagination and conscience. Neo-Platonism drew both form and substance from a system of abstract thought. Its gods were still-born, being generated by logical dichotomy. Only in the lower purlieus of the system, filled in by accepting current superstitions, was there any contact with something like vital religious forces. But those minor elements — hopes and fears about another world, fasts and penances, ecstasies and marvels — had no necessary relation to that metaphysical system. Such practices could be found in every religion, in every philosophical sect of the time. The Alexandrian dialectic of the supernatural accordingly remained a mere schema or skeleton, to be filled in with the materials of some real religion, if such a religion should arise. As such a schema the Neo-Platonic system actually passed over to Christian theology, furnishing the latter with its categories, its language, and its speculative method. But that dialectic served in Christianity to give form to a religious substance furnished by Hebrew and apostolic tradition, a religious substance such as, after the Pagan religion was discredited, Neo-Platonism necessarily lacked and was powerless to generate.

We have mentioned apostolic tradition. It is fortunately not requisite for our purpose to discuss the origin of this tradition, much less to decide how much of what the Christian Church eventually taught might be traced to its Founder. That is a point which even the most thorough scholars seem still to decide mainly by their prejudices, perhaps because other material is lacking on which to base a decision. For our present object we may admit the most extreme hypotheses as equally possible. The whole body of Catholic doctrine may have been contained in the oral teaching of Christ; or, on the other hand, a historical Jesus may not have existed at all, or may have been one among many obscure Jewish revolutionists, the one who, by accident, came afterward to be regarded as the initiator of a movement to which all sorts of forces contributed, and with which he had really had nothing to do. In either case the fact remains which alone interests us here; that after three or four centuries of confused struggles, an institution emerged which called itself the Catholic Church. This church, possessed of a recognized hierarchy and a recognized dogma, triumphed, both over the ancient religion, which it called Paganism, and over its many collateral rivals, which it called heresies. Why did it triumph? What was there in its novel dogma and practice that enchained the minds that Paganism could retain no longer, and that would not be content with Neo-Platonism, native, philosophical, and pliable as that system was?

The answer, to be adequate, would have to be long; but perhaps we may indicate the spirit in which it ought to be conceived. Paganism was a religion, but was discarded because it was not supernatural: Neo-Platonism could not be maintained because it was not a religion. Christianity was both. It had its roots in a national faith, moulded by the trials and passions of a singularly religious people; that connection with Judaism gave Christianity a foothold in history, a definite dogmatic nucleus, which it was a true instinct in the Church never to abandon, much as certain speculative heresies might cry out against the unnatural union of a theory of redemption with one of creation, and of a world-denying ascetic idealism, which Christianity was essentially, with the national laws, the crude deism, and the strenuous worldliness of the ancient Jews. However, had the Gnostic or Manichæan heresies been victorious, Christianity would have been reduced to a floating speculation: its hard kernel of positive dogma, of Scripture, and of hieratic tradition would have been dissolved. It would have ceased to represent antiquity or to hand down an ancestral piety: in fine, by its eagerness to express itself as a perfect philosophy, it would have ceased to be a religion. How essential an element its Hebraism was, we can see now by the study of Protestantism, a group of heresies in which the practical instincts and sentimental needs of the Teutonic race found expression, by throwing over more or less completely the Catholic dogma and ritual. Yet in this revolution the Protestants maintained, or rather increased, the intensity of their religious consciousness, chiefly by absorbing the elements of Hebrew law and prophecy which they could find in the Bible and casting into that traditional form their personal conscience or their national ideals.

How inadequate, on the other hand, this Hebraic

element would have been to constitute the supernatural religion that was now needed, appears very
clearly from the case of Philo Judæus. Here was
a man, heir to all the piety and fervour of his race,
who at the same time was a Neo-Platonist three
hundred years before Plotinus and, as it were, the
first Father of the Church. But his religion, being national, was not communicable and, being
positivistic, was at fundamental odds with the
spirit of his philosophy. It remained, therefore,
as a merely personal treasure and heirloom, the
possession of his private life: his disciples, had
he had any, must either have been Jews themselves or else must have been the followers merely
of his philosophy. His religion could not have
passed to them; they would have regarded it, as
we might regard the Christianity of Kant or the
wife-worship of Comte, as a private circumstance,
a detached trait, less damaging, perhaps, to his
philosophy than favourable to his loyal heart.

Philo, in his commentaries on the Bible, sought
to envelop and transform every detail in the
light of Platonic metaphysics. His interpretations are often violent, but the ingenuous artifice
of them would have delighted his contemporaries
as much as himself, and was adopted afterward by
all the Fathers and theologians of the Church.
Philo's theology was thus a success, even a model;
yet he failed, because of the inadequacy of his

religion. What interest, what relevance, could it
have for any Gentile to hear about the deliverance
of Israel out of Egypt or out of Babylon, or about
circumcision and prescribed meats, or about the
sacrifices in the Temple ? What charm or credibility could he find in further promises of glorious
kingdoms, flowing with milk and honey ?   Such
images might later appeal to the imagination of
New England Puritans and make a religion for
them : but what meaning could they have to the
weary Pagan ?   No doubt the Jews carried with
them an ideal of righteousness and prosperity ;
but the Gentile was sick of heroes and high priests
and founders of cities.   Stoic virtues were as vain
in his eyes as Sybaritic joys.   He did not wish
his passions to be flattered, not even his pride or
the passion for a social Utopia.   He wished his
passions to be mortified and his soul to be re-
deemed.   He would not look for a Messiah, unless
he could find him on a cross.

That is the essence of the matter.   What overcame the world, because it was what the world
desired, was not a moral reform — for that was
preached by every sect ; not an ascetic regimen —
for that was practised by heathen gymnosophists
and Pagan philosophers ; not brotherly love within
the Church — for the Jews had and have that at
least in equal measure ; but what overcame the
world was what Saint Paul said he would always

preach : Christ and him crucified.   Therein was a
new poetry, a new ideal, a new God.   Therein was
the transcript of the real experience of humanity,
as men found it in their inmost souls and as they
were dimly aware of it in universal history.   The
moving power was a fable — for who stopped to
question whether its elements were historical, if
only its meaning were profound and its inspiration
contagious ?   This fable had points of attachment
to real life in a visible brotherhood and in an extant
worship, as well as in the religious past of a whole
people.   At the same time it carried the imagination into a new sphere ; it sanctified the poverty
and sorrow at which Paganism had shuddered ; it
awakened tenderer emotions, revealed more human
objects of adoration, and furnished subtler instru-
ments of grace.   It was a whole world of poetry
descended among men, like the angels at the
Nativity, doubling, as it were, their habitation, so
that they might move through supernatural realms
in the spirit while they walked the earth in the
flesh.   The consciousness of new loves, new duties,
fresh consolations, and luminous unutterable hopes
accompanied them wherever they went.   They
stopped willingly in the midst of their business for
recollection, like men in love ; they sought to
stimulate their imaginations, to focus, as it were,
the long vistas of an invisible landscape.

If the importunity of affairs or of ill-subdued pas-

sions disturbed that dream, they could still return
to it at leisure in the solitude of some shrine or
under the spell of some canticle or of some sacramental image; and meantime they could keep their
faith in reserve as their secret and their resource.
The longer the vision lasted and the steadier it became, the more closely, of course, was it intertwined
with daily acts and common affections; and as real
life gradually enriched that vision with its suggestions, so religion in turn gradually coloured common
life with its unearthly light.   In the saint, in the
soul that had become already the perpetual citizen of
that higher sphere, nothing in this world remained
without reference to the other, nor was anything
done save for a supernatural end.   Thus the redemption was actually accomplished and the soul
was lifted above the conditions of this life, so that
death itself could bring but a slight and unessential
change of environment.

Morbid as this species of faith may seem, visionary as it certainly was, it is not to be confused
with an arbitrary madness or with personal illusions.   Two circumstances raised this imaginative
piety to a high dignity and made it compatible with
great accomplishments, both in thought and in action.
In the first place the religious world constituted a
system complete and consistent within itself.   There
was occasion within it for the exercise of reason,
for the awakening and discipline of emotion, for

the exertion of effort.   As music, for all that it contains nothing of a material or practical nature, offers a field for the development of human faculty and presents laws and conditions which, within its sphere, must be obeyed and which reward obedience with the keenest and purest pleasures; so a supernatural religion, when it is traditional and systematic like Christianity, offers another world, almost as vast and solid as the real one, in which the soul may develop.   In entering it we do not enter a sphere of arbitrary dreams, but a sphere of law where learning, experience, and happiness may be gained.   There is more method, more reason, in such madness than in the sanity of most people. The world of the Christian imagination was eminently a field for moral experience; moral ideas were there objectified into supernatural forces, and instead of being obscured as in the real world by irrational accidents formed an intelligible cosmos, vast, massive, and steadfast.   For this reason the believer in any adequate and mature supernatural religion clings to it with such strange tenacity and regards it as his highest heritage, while the outsider, whose imagination speaks another language or is dumb altogether, wonders how so wild a fiction can take root in a reasonable mind.

The other circumstance that ennobled the Christian system was that all its parts had some sig-

nificance and poetic truth, although they contained,
or needed to contain, nothing empirically real.
The system was a great poem which, besides being
well constructed in itself, was allegorical of actual
experience, and contained, as in a hieroglyph, a
very deep knowledge of the world and of the
human mind.   For what was the object that un-
folded itself before the Christian imagination, the
vision that converted and regenerated the world ?
It was a picture of human destiny.   It was an epic,
containing, as it were, the moral autobiography of
man.   The object of Pagan religion and philosophy
had been a picture of the material cosmos, conceived as a vast animal and inhabited by a multitude of individual spirits.   Even the Neo-Platonists
thought of nothing else, much as they might multiply abstract names for its principles and fancifully
confuse them with the spheres.   It was always a
vast, living, physical engine, a cosmos of life in
which man had a determinate province.   His
spirit, losing its personality, might be absorbed
into the ethereal element from which it came; but
this emanation and absorption was itself an unchanging process, the systole and diastole of the
universal heart.   Practical religion consisted in
honouring the nearest gods and accepting from
them man's apportioned goods, not without looking, perhaps, with a reverence that needed no
ritual, to the enveloping whole that prescribed to

gods and men their respective functions. Thus
even Neo-Platonism represented man as a minor
incident in the universe, supernatural though that
universe might be. The spiritual spheres were
only the invisible repetitions of the visible, as the
Platonic ideas from the beginning had been only
a dialectic reduplication of the objects in this
world. It was against this allotment that the
soul was rebelling. It was looking for a deliverance that should be not so much the consciousness of something higher as the hope of something better.

Now, the great characteristic of Christianity,
inherited from Judaism, was that its scheme was
historical. Not existences but events were the
subject of its primary interest. It presented a
story, not a cosmology. It was an epic in which
there was, of course, superhuman machinery, but
of which the subject was man, and, notable circumstance, the Hero was a man as well. Like
Buddhism, it gave the highest honour to a man
who could lead his fellow-men to perfection. What
had previously been the divine reality — the engine
of Nature — now became a temporary stage, built
for the exigencies of a human drama. What had
been before a detail of the edifice — the life of
man — now became the argument and purpose
of the whole creation. Notable transformation, on
which the philosopher cannot meditate too much.

Was Christianity right in saying that the world was made for man? Was the account it adopted of the method and causes of Creation conceivably correct? Was the garden of Eden a historical reality, and were the Hebrew prophecies announcements of the advent of Jesus Christ? Did the deluge come because of man's wickedness, and will the last day coincide with the dramatic dénouement of the Church's history? In other words, is the spiritual experience of man the explanation of the universe? Certainly not, if we are thinking of a scientific, not of a poetical explanation. As a matter of fact, man is a product of laws which must also destroy him, and which, as Spinoza would say, infinitely exceed him in their scope and power. His welfare is indifferent to the stars, but dependent on them. And yet that counter-Copernican revolution accomplished by Christianity — a revolution which Kant should hardly have attributed to himself — which put man in the centre of the universe and made the stars circle about him, must have some kind of justification. And indeed its justification (if we may be so brief on so great a subject) is that what is false in the science of facts may be true in the science of values. While the existence of things must be understood by referring them to their causes, which are mechanical, their functions can only be explained by what is interesting in their results,

in other words, by their relation to human nature
and to human happiness.

The Christian drama was a magnificent poetic
rendering of this side of the matter, a side which
Socrates had envisaged by his admirable method,
but which now flooded the consciousness of mankind with torrential emotions. Christianity was
born under an eclipse, when the light of Nature
was obscured; but the star that intercepted that
light was itself luminous, and shed on succeed-
ing ages a moonlike radiance, paler and sadder
than the other, but no less divine, and meriting
no less to be eternal. Man now studied his own
destiny, as he had before studied the sky, and
the woods, and the sunny depths of water; and
as the earlier study produced in his soul — *anima
naturaliter poeta* — the images of Zeus, Pan, and
Nereus, so the later study produced the images of
Jesus and of Mary, of Heaven and Hell, of miracles
and sacraments. The observation was no less exact,
the translation into poetic images no less wonderful
here than there. To trace the endless transfigura-
tion, with all its unconscious ingenuity and harmony, might be the theme of a fascinating science.
Let not the reader fancy that in Christianity everything was settled by records and traditions. The
idea of Christ himself had to be constructed by the
imagination in response to moral demands, tradition giving only the barest external points of

attachment. The facts were nothing until they became symbols; and nothing could turn them into symbols except an eager imagination on the watch for all that might embody its dreams.

The crucifixion, for example, would remain a tragic incident without further significance, if we regard it merely as a historical fact; to make it a religious mystery, an idea capable of converting the world, the moral imagination must transform it into something that happens for the sake of the soul, so that each believer may say to himself that Christ so suffered for the love of him. And such a thought is surely the objectification of an inner impulse; the idea of Christ becomes something spiritual, something poetical. What literal meaning could there be in saying that one man or one God died for the sake of each and every other individual? By what effective causal principle could their salvation be thought to necessitate his death, or his death to make possible their salvation? By an ὕστερον πρότερον natural to the imagination; for in truth the matter is reversed. Christ's death is a symbol of human life. Men could "believe in" his death, because it was a figure and premonition of the burden of their experience. That is why, when some Apostle told them the story, they could say to him: "Sir, I perceive that thou art a prophet: thou hast told me all things whatsoever I have felt." Thus the central fact of all Christ's history, narrated by every Evangelist, could still be nothing but a painful incident, as unessential to the Christian religion as the death of Socrates to the Socratic philosophy, were it not transformed by the imagination of the believer into the counterpart of his own moral need. Then, by ceasing to be viewed as a historical fact, the death of Christ becomes a religious inspiration. The whole of Christian doctrine is thus religious and efficacious only when it becomes poetry, because only then is it the felt counterpart of personal experience and a genuine expansion of human life.

Take, as another example, the doctrine of eternal rewards and punishments. Many perplexed Christians of our day try to reconcile this spirited fable with their modern horror of physical suffering and their detestation of cruelty; and it must be admitted that the image of men suffering unending tortures in retribution for a few ignorant and sufficiently wretched sins is, even as poetry, somewhat repellent. The idea of torments and vengeance is happily becoming alien to our society and is therefore not a natural vehicle for our religion. Some accordingly reject altogether the Christian doctrine on this point, which is too strong for their nerves. Their objection, of course, is not simply that there is no evidence of its truth. If they asked for evidence, would they believe anything? Proofs are the last thing looked for by a truly religious mind which feels the imaginative fitness of its faith and knows instinctively that, in such a matter, imaginative fitness is all that can be required. The reason men reject the doctrine of eternal punishment is that they find it distasteful or unmeaning. They show, by the nature of their objections, that they acknowledge poetic propriety or moral truth to be the sole criterion of religious credibility.

But, passing over the change of sentiment which gives rise to this change of doctrine, let us inquire of what reality Christian eschatology was the imaginative rendering. What was it in the actual life of men that made them think of themselves as hanging between eternal bliss and eternal perdition? Was it not the diversity, the momentousness, and the finality of their experience here? No doubt the desire to make the reversal of the injustices of this world as melodramatic and picturesque as possible contributed to the adoption of this idea; the ideal values of life were thus contrasted with its apparent values in the most absolute and graphic manner. But we may say that beneath this motive, based on the exigences of exposition and edification, there was a deeper intuition. There was the genuine moralist's sympathy with a philosophic and logical view of immortality rather than with a superstitious and sentimental one. Another life

exists and is infinitely more important than this
life; but it is reached by the intuition of ideals,
not by the multiplication of phenomena; it is
an eternal state not an indefinite succession of
changes. Transitory life ends for the Christian
when the balance-sheet of his individual merits
and demerits is made up, and the eternity that
ensues is the eternal reality of those values.

For the Oriental, who believed in transmigration, the individual dissolved into an infinity of
phases; he went on actually and perpetually, as
Nature does; his immortality was a long Purgatory behind which a shadowy Hell and Heaven
scarcely appeared in the form of annihilation or
absorption. This happened because the Oriental
mind has no middle; it oscillates between ex-
tremes and passes directly from sense to mysticism, and back again; it lacks virile understanding
and intelligence creative of form. But Christianity,
following in this the Socratic philosophy, rose to
the conception of eternal essences, forms suspended
above the flux of natural things and expressing
the ideal suggestions and rational goals of experience. Each man, for Christianity, has an immortal soul; each life has the potentiality of an eternal
meaning, and as this potentiality is or is not actu-
alized, as this meaning is or is not expressed in
the phenomena of this life, the soul is eternally
saved or lost. As the tree falleth, so it lieth.

The finality of this brief and personal experiment, the consequent awful solemnity of the hour of death when all trial is over and when the eternal sentence is passed, has always been duly felt by the Christian. The Church, indeed, in answer to the demand for a more refined and discriminating presentation of its dogma, introduced the temporary discipline of Purgatory, in which the virtues already stamped on the soul might be brought to greater clearness and rid of the alloy of imperfection; but this purification allowed no essential development, no change of character or fate; the soul in Purgatory was already saved, already holy.

The harshness of the doctrine of eternal judgment is therefore a consequence of its symbolic truth. The Church might have been less absolute in the matter had she yielded more, as she did in the doctrine of Purgatory, to the desire for merely imaginary extensions of human experience. But her better instincts kept her, after all, to the moral interpretation of reality; and the facts to be rendered were uncompromising enough. Art is long, life brief. To have told men they would have infinite opportunities to reform and to advance would have been to feed them on gratuitous fictions without raising them, as it was the function of Christianity to do, to a consciousness of the spiritual meaning and upshot of existence. To have speculated about the infinite extent of experience and its

H

endless transformations, after the manner of the
barbarous religions, and never to have conceived
its moral essence, would have been to encourage a
dream which may by chance be prophetic, but
which is as devoid of ideal meaning as of empirical
probability. Christian fictions were at least significant; they beguiled the intellect, no doubt, and
were mistaken for accounts of external fact; but
they enlightened the imagination; they made man
understand, as never before or since, the pathos and
nobility of his life, the necessity of discipline, the
possibility of sanctity, the transcendence and the humanity of the divine. For the divine was reached
by the idealization of the human. The supernatural was an allegory of the natural, and rendered
the values of transitory things under the image of
eternal existences. Thus the finality of our activity
in this world, together with the eternity of its ideal
meanings, was admirably rendered by the Christian
dogma of a final judgment.

But there was another moral truth which was
impressed upon the believer by that doctrine and
which could not be enforced in any other way without presupposing in him an unusual philosophic
acumen and elevation of mind. That is the truth
that moral distinctions are absolute. A cool philosophy suffices to show us that moral distinctions
exist, since men prefer some experiences to others
and can by their action bring these good and evil

experiences upon themselves and upon their fellows. But a survey of Nature may at the same time impress us with the fact that these goods and evils are singularly mixed, that there is hardly an advantage gained which is not bought by some loss, or any loss which is not an opportunity for the attainment of some advantage. While it would be chimerical to pretend that such compensation was always adequate, and that, in consequence, no one condition was ever really preferable to any other, yet the perplexities into which moral aspiration is thrown by these contradictory vistas is often productive of the desire to reach some other point of view, to escape into what is irrationally thought to be a higher category than the moral. The serious consideration of those things which are right according to human reason and interest may then yield to a fanatical reliance on some facile general notion.

It may be thought, for instance, that what is regular or necessary or universal is therefore right and good; thus a dazed contemplation of the actual may take the place of the determination of the ideal. Mysticism in regard to the better and the worse, by which good and bad are woven into a seamless garment of sorry magnificence in which the whole universe is wrapped up, is like mysticism on other subjects; it consists in the theoretic renunciation of a natural attitude, in this case of the natural attitude of welcome and repulsion in

the presence of various things. But this category
is the most fundamental of all those that the
human mind employs, and it cannot be surrendered so long as life endures. It is indeed the
conscious echo of those vital instincts by whose
operation we exist. Levity and mysticism may do
all they can — and they can do much — to make
men think moral distinctions unauthoritative, because moral distinctions may be either ignored or
transcended. Yet the essential assertion that one
thing is really better than another remains involved
in every act of every living being. It is involved
even in the operation of abstract thinking, where
a cogent conclusion, being still coveted, is assumed
to be a good, or in that æsthetic and theoretic enthusiasm before cosmic laws, which is the human
foundation of this mysticism itself.

It is accordingly a moral truth which no subter-
fuge can elude, that some things are really better
than others. In the daily course of affairs we are
constantly in the presence of events which by turning out one way or the other produce a real, an
irrevocable, increase of good or evil in the world.
The complexities of life, struggling as it does
amidst irrational forces, may make the attainment
of one good the cause of the unattainableness of
another; they cannot destroy the essential desirability of both. The niggardliness of Nature cannot sterilize the ideal; the odious circumstances

which make the attainment of many goods conditional on the perpetration of some evil, and which punish every virtue by some incapacity or some abuse, — these odious circumstances cannot rob any good of its natural sweetness, nor all goods together of their conceptual harmony. To the heart that has felt it and that is the true judge, every loss is irretrievable and every joy indestructible. Eventual compensations may obliterate the memory of these values but cannot destroy their reality. The future can only furnish further applications of the principle by which they arose and were justified.

Now, how utter this moral truth imaginatively, how clothe it in an image that might render its absoluteness and its force? Could any method be better than to say: Your eternal destiny is hanging in the balance: the grace of God, the influences of others, and your own will reacting upon both are shaping at every moment issues of absolute importance. What happens here and now decides not merely incidental pains and pleasures — which perhaps a brave and careless spirit might alike despise — but helps to determine your eternal destiny of joy or anguish, and the eternal destiny of your neighbour. In place of the confused vistas of the empirical world, in which the threads of benefit and injury might seem to be mingled and lost, the imagination substituted the clear vision of Hell and Heaven; while the determination of our destiny was made to depend upon obedience to recognized duties.

Now these duties may often have been far from corresponding to those which reason would impose; but the intention and the principle at least were sound. It was felt that the actions and passions of this world breed momentous values, values which being ideal are as infinite as values can be in the estimation of reason — the values of truth, of love, of rationality, of perfection — although both the length of the experience in which they arise and the number of persons who share that experience may be extremely limited. But the mechanical measure of experience in length, intensity, or multiplication has nothing to do with its moral significance in realizing truth or virtue. Therefore the difference in dignity between the satisfactions of reason and the satisfactions of sense is fittingly rendered by the infinite disproportion between heavenly and earthly joys. In our imaginative translation we are justified in saying that the alternative between infinite happiness and infinite misery is yawning before us, because the alternative between rational failure or success is actually present. The decisions we make from moment to moment, on which the ideal value of our life and character depends, actually constitute in a few years a decision which is irrevocable.

The Christian doctrine of rewards and punishments is thus in harmony with moral truths which a different doctrine might have obscured. The good souls that wish to fancy that everybody will be ultimately saved, subject a fable to standards appropriate to matters of fact, and thereby deprive the fable of that moral significance which is its excuse for being. If every one is ultimately saved, there is nothing truly momentous about alternative events: all paths lead more or less circuitously to the same end. The only ground which then remains for discriminating the better from the worse is the pleasantness or unpleasantness of the path to salvation. All moral meanings inhere, then, in this life, and the other life is without significance. Heaven comes to replace life empirically without fulfilling it ideally. We are reduced for our moral standards to phenomenal values, to the worth of life in transitory feeling. These values are quite real, but they are not those which poetry and religion have for their object. They are values present to sense, not to reason and imagination.

The ideal of a supervening general bliss presents indeed an abstract desideratum, but not the ideal involved in the actual forces of life; that end would have no rational relation to its primary factors; it would not be built on our instinctive preferences but would abolish them by a miraculous dream, following alike upon every species of activity. Moral differences would have existed merely to be forgotten; for if we say they were remembered, but transcended and put to rest, we plunge into an even worse contradiction to the conscience and the will. For if we say that the universal bliss consists in the assurance, mystically received, that while individual experiences may differ in value they all equally conduce to the perfection of the universe, we deny not merely the momentousness but even the elementary validity of moral distinctions. We assert that the best idea of God is that least like the ideal of man, and that the nearer we come to the vision of truth the farther we are from the feeling of preference. In our attempt to extend the good we thus abolish its essence. Our religion consists in denying the authority of the ideal, which is its only rational foundation; and thus that religion, while gaining nothing in empirical reality, comes to express a moral falsehood instead of a moral truth.

If we looked in religion for an account of facts, as most people do, we should have to pass a very different judgment on these several views. The mechanical world is a connected system and Nature seems to be dynamically one; the intuitions on which mysticism feeds are therefore true intuitions. The expectation of a millennium is on the other hand quite visionary, because the evidence of history, while it shows undeniable progress in many directions, shows that this progress is essentially relative, partial, and transitory. As for the Christian doctrine of the judgment, it is something wholly out of relation to empirical facts, it assumes the existence of a supernatural sphere, and is beyond the reach of scientific evidence of any kind. But if we look on religion as on a kind of poetry, as we have decided here to do, — as on a kind of poetry that expresses moral values and reacts beneficently upon life, — we shall see that the Christian doctrine is alone justified. For mysticism is not an imaginative construction at all but a renunciation or confusion of our faculties; here a surrender of the human ideal in the presence of a mechanical force that is felt, and correctly felt, to tend to vaguer results or rather to tend to nothing in particular. Mysticism is not a religion but a religious disease. The idea of universal salvation, on the other hand, is the expression of a feeble sentimentality, a pleasant reverie without structure or significance. But the doctrine of eternal rewards and punishments is, as we have tried to show, an expression of moral truth, a poetic rendering of the fact that rational values are ideal, momentous, and irreversible.

It would be easy to multiply examples and to exhibit the various parts of Christianity as so many interpretations of human life in its ideal aspects.

But we are not attempting to narrate facts so much as to advance an idea, and the illustrations given will perhaps suffice to make our conception intelligible. There is, however, a possible misunderstanding which we should be careful to avoid in this dangerous field of philosophic interpretation. In saying that a given religion was the poetic transformation of an experience, we must not imagine that it was thought to be such — for it is evident that every sincere Christian believed in the literal and empirical reality of all that the Christian epic contained. Nor should we imagine that philosophic ideas, or general reflections on life, were the origin of religion, and that afterward certain useful myths, known to be such by their authors, were mistaken for history and for literal prophecy. That sometimes happens, when historians, poets, or philosophers are turned by the unintelligent veneration of posterity into religious prophets. Such was the fate of Plato, for instance, or of the writer of the "Song of Solomon"; but no great and living religion was ever founded in that way.

Had Christianity or any other religion had its basis in literary or philosophical allegories, it would never have become a religion, because the poetry of it would never have been interwoven with the figures and events of real life. No tomb, no relic, no material miracle, no personal derivation of authority, would have existed to serve as the nucleus of devotion and the point of junction between this world and the other. The origin of Christian dogma lay in historic facts and in doctrines literally meant by their authors. It is one of the greatest possible illusions in these matters to fancy that the meaning which we see in parables and mysteries was the meaning they had in the beginning, but which later misinterpretation had obscured. On the contrary — as a glance at any incipient religious movement now going on will show us — the authors of doctrines, however obvious it may be to every one else that these doctrines have only a figurative validity, are the first dupes to their own intuitions. This is no less true of metaphysical theories than of spontaneous superstitions: did their promulgator understand the character of their justification he would give himself out for a simple poet, appeal only to cultivated minds, and never turn his energies to stimulating private delusions, not to speak of public fanaticisms. The best philosophers seldom perceive the poetic merit of their systems.

So among the ancients it was not an abstract observation of Nature, with conscious allegory supervening, that was the origin of mythology, but the interpretation was spontaneous, the illusion was radical, a consciousness of the god's presence was the first impression produced by the phenomenon. Else, in this case too, poetry would never have become superstition; what made it superstition was the initial incapacity in people to discriminate the objects of imagination from those of the understanding. The fancy thus attached its images, without distinguishing their ideal locus, to the visible world, and men became superstitious not because they had too much imagination, but because they were not aware that they had any.

In what sense, then, are we justified in saying that religion expresses moral ideals ? In the sense that moral significance, while not the source of religions, is the criterion of their value and the reason why they may deserve to endure. Far as the conception of an allegory may be from the minds of prophets, yet the prophecy can only take root in the popular imagination if it recommends itself to some human interest. There must be some correspondence between the doctrine announced or the hopes set forth, and the natural demands of the human spirit. Otherwise, although the new faith might be preached, it would not be accepted. The significance of religious doctrines has therefore been the condition of their spread, their maintenance, and their development, although not the condition of their origin. In Darwinian language, moral significance has been a spontaneous variation of superstition, and this variation has insured its survival as a religion. For religion differs from superstition not psychologically but morally, not in its origin but in its worth. This worth, when actually felt and appreciated, becomes of course a dynamic factor and contributes like other psychological elements to the evolution of events; but being a logical harmony, a rational beauty, this worth is only appreciable by a few minds, and those the least primitive and the least capable of guiding popular movements. Reason is powerless to found religions, although it is alone competent to judge them. Good religions are therefore the product of unconscious rationality, of imaginative impulses fortunately moral.

Particularly does this appear in the early history of Christianity. Every shade of heresy, every kind of mixture of Christian and other elements was tried and found advocates; but after a greater or less success they all disappeared, leaving only the Church standing. For the Church had known how to combine those dogmas and practices in which the imagination of the time, and to a great extent of all times, might find fitting expression. Imaginative significance was the touchstone of orthodoxy; tradition itself was tested by this standard. By this standard the canon of Scripture was fixed, so as neither to exclude the Old Testament, which the pure metaphysicians would have rejected, nor to accept every gospel that circulated under the name of an apostle, and which might

please a wonder-loving and detail-loving piety.
By the same criterion the ritual was composed,
the dogma developed, the nature of Christ defined,
the sacraments and discipline of the Church regu-
lated. The result was a comprehensive system
where, under the shadow of a great epic, which
expanded and interpreted the history of mankind
from the Creation to the Day of Doom, a place
was found for as many religious instincts and as
many religious traditions as possible; while at the
same time the dialectic proficiency of an age that
inherited the discipline of Greek philosophy, introduced into the system a great consistency and a
great metaphysical subtlety. Time mellowed and
expanded these dogmas, bringing them into relation with the needs of a multiform piety; a justification was found both for asceticism and for a
virtuous naturalism, both for contemplation and
for action; and thus it became possible for the
Church to insinuate her sanctions and her spirit
into the motives of men, and to embody the religion
of many nations during many ages.

The Church's successes, however, were not all
legitimate; they were not everywhere due to a
real correspondence between her forms and the
ideal life of men. It was only the inhabitants of
the Græco-Roman world that were quite prepared
to understand her. When the sword, or the authority of a higher worldly civilization, carried her

influence beyond the borders of the Roman Empire we may observe that her authority seldom proved stable. She was felt, by those peoples whose imaginative traditions and whose moral experience she did not express, to be something alien and artificial. The Teutonic races finally threw off what they felt to be her yoke. If they reconstructed their religion out of elements which she had furnished, that was only because religion is bound to be traditional, and they had been Christians for many hundred years. A wholly new philosophy or poetry could not have taken immediate root in their minds; even the philosophy which Germany has since produced, when the national spirit was reaching, so to speak, its majority, hardly seems able to constitute an independent religion, but takes shelter under some form of Christianity, however much the spirit of that religion may be transformed.

At first, indeed, the new movement took the Bible for its starting-point. So heterogeneous a book, which was already habitually interpreted in so many fanciful ways, was indeed an admirable basis for the imagination to build upon. The self-reliant and dreamy Teuton could spin out of the Biblical chronicles and rhapsodies convictions after his own heart; while his fixed persuasion that the Bible was the word of God, was strengthened (not illegitimately) by his ability to

make it express his own moral ideals. The in
tensity of his religion was proportionate to the
degree in which he had made it the imaginative
rendering of his own character.

Protestantism in its vital elements was thus a
perfectly new, a perfectly spontaneous religion.
The illusion that it was a return to primitive
Christianity was useful for controversial purposes
and helped to justify the iconoclastic passions of
the time; but this illusion did not touch the true
essence of Protestantism, nor the secret of its legitimacy and power as a religion. This was its new
embodiment of human ideals in imaginative forms,
whereby those ideals became explicit and found a
remarkable expression in action. These ideals
were quite Teutonic and looked to inner spontaneity and outward prosperity; they were more
allied to those of the Hebrews than to those of
the early Christians, whose religion was all miracles, asceticism, and withdrawal from the world.
Indeed we may say that the typical Protestant
was himself his own church and made the selection and interpretation of tradition according to
the demands of his personal spirit. What the
Fathers did for the Church in the fourth century,
the Reformers did for themselves in the sixteenth,
and have continued to do on the occasion of their
various appearances.

If we judge this interpretation by poetic standards, we cannot resist the conclusion that the old version was infinitely superior. The Protestant, with his personal resources, was reduced to making grotesquely and partially that translation of moral life which the Fathers had made comprehensively and beautifully, inspired as they were by all the experience of antiquity and all the hopes of youthful Christendom. Nevertheless, Protestantism has the unmistakable character of a genuine religion, a character which tradition passively accepted and dogma, regarded as so much external truth, may easily lose; it is in correspondence with the actual ideals and instincts of the believer; it is the self-assertion of a living soul. Its meagreness and eccentricity are simply evidences of its personal basis. It is in full harmony with the practical impulses it comes to sanction, and accordingly it gains in efficiency all that it loses in dignity and truth.

The principle by which the Christian system had developed, although reapplied by the Protestants to their own inner life, was not understood by them in its historical applications. They had little sympathy with the spiritual needs and habits of that Pagan society in which Christianity had grown up. That society had found in Christianity a sort of last love, a rejuvenating supersensible hope, and had bequeathed to the Gospel of Redemption, for its better embodiment and ornament, all its own

I

wealth of art, philosophy, and devotion. This
embodiment of Christianity represented a civilization through which the Teutonic races had
not passed and which they never could have produced; it appealed to a kind of imagination and
sentiment which was foreign to them. This embodiment, accordingly, was the object of their first
and fiercest attack, really because it was unsympathetic to their own temperament but ostensibly
because they could not find its basis in those
Hebraic elements of Christianity which make up
the greater bulk of the Bible. They did not value
the sublime aspiration of Christianity to be not
something Hebraic or Teutonic but something
Catholic and human; and they blamed everything
which went beyond the accidental limits of their
own sympathies and the narrow scope of their own
experience.

Yet it was only by virtue of this complement
inherited from Paganism, or at least supplied by
the instincts and traditions on which Paganism
had reposed, that Christianity could claim to
approach a humane universality or to achieve an
imaginative adequacy. The problem was to compose, in the form of a cosmic epic, with metaphysical justifications and effectual starting-points
for moral action, the spiritual autobiography of
man. The central idea of this composition was
to be the idea of a Redemption. Around this were

to be gathered and moulded together elements drawn from Hebrew tradition and scripture, others furnished by Paganism, together with all that the living imagination of the time could create. Nor was it right or fitting to make a merely theoretical or ethical synthesis. Doctrine must find its sensible echo in worship, in art, in the feasts and fasts of the year. Only when thus permeating life and expressing itself to every sense and faculty can a religion be said to have reached completion; only then has the imagination exhausted its means of utterance.

The great success which Christianity achieved in this immense undertaking makes it, after classic antiquity, the most important phase in the history of mankind. It is clear, however, that this success was not complete. That fallacy from which the Pagan religion alone has been free, that πρῶτον ψεῦδος of all fanaticism, the natural but hopeless misunderstanding of imagining that poetry in order to be religion, in order to be the inspiration of life, must first deny that it is poetry and deceive us about the facts with which we have to deal — this misunderstanding has marred the work of the Christian imagination and condemned it, if we may trust appearances, to be transitory. For by this misunderstanding Christian doctrine was brought into conflict with reality, of which it pretends to prejudge the character, and also into

conflict with what might have been its own elements, with all excluded religious instincts and
imaginative ideals. Human life is always essentially the same, and therefore a religion which, like
Christianity, seizes the essence of that life, ought
to be an eternal religion. But it may forfeit that
privilege by entangling itself with a particular
account of matters of fact, matters irrelevant to its
ideal significance, and further by intrenching itself,
by virtue of that entanglement, in an inadequate
regimen or a too narrow imaginative development,
thus putting its ideal authority in jeopardy by
opposing it to other intuitions and practices no
less religious than its own.

Can Christianity escape these perils? Can it
reform its claims, or can it overwhelm all opposition and take the human heart once more by
storm? The future alone can decide. The greatest calamity, however, would be that which seems,
alas! not unlikely to befall our immediate posterity, namely, that while Christianity should be
discredited no other religion, more disillusioned
and not less inspired, should come to take its
place. Until the imagination should have time to
recover and to reassert its legitimate and kindly
power, the European races would then be reduced to confessing that while they had mastered
the mechanical forces of Nature, both by science
and by the arts, they had become incapable of

mastering or understanding themselves, and that,
bewildered like the beasts by the revolutions of the
heavens and by their own irrational passions, they
could find no way of uttering the ideal meaning of
their life.

V

V

PLATONIC LOVE IN SOME ITALIAN POETS

When the fruits of philosophic reflection, condensed into some phrase, pass into the common language of men, there does not and there cannot accompany them any just appreciation of their meaning or of the long experience and travail of soul from which they have arisen. Few doctrines have suffered more by popularization than the intuitions of Plato. The public sees in Platonic sayings little more than phrases employed by unpractical minds to cloak the emptiness of their yearnings. Finding these fragments of an obsolete speech put to bad uses, we are apt to ignore and despise them, much as a modern peasant might despise the fragment of a frieze or a metope which he found built into his cottage wall. It is not only the works of plastic art that moulder and disintegrate to furnish materials for the barbarous masons of a later age: the great edifices of reason also crumble, their plan is lost, and their fragments, picked where they happen to lie, become the materials of a feebler thought. In common speech we find such bits of ancient wisdom embedded; they prove the intelligence of some ancestor of ours, but are no evidence of our own. When used in ignorance of their meaning, they become misplaced flourishes, lapses into mystery in the businesslike plainness of our thought.

Yet there is one man, the archæologist, to whom nothing is so interesting as just these stones which a practical builder would have rejected. He forgives the ignorance and barbarism that placed them where they are; he is absorbed in studying their sculptured surface and delighted if his fancy can pass from them to the idea of the majestic whole to which they once belonged. So in the presence of a much-abused philosophic phrase, we may be interested in reconstructing the experience which once gave it meaning and form. Words are at least the tombs of ideas, and the most conventional formulas of poets or theologians are still good subjects for the archæologist of passion. He may find a treasure there; or at any rate he may hope to be rewarded for his labour by the ideal restoration of some once beautiful temple of Athena.

Something of this kind is what we may now attempt to do with regard to one or two Platonic ideas, ideas which under the often ironical title of Platonic love, are constantly referred to and

seldom understood. These ideas may be defined
as the transformation of the appreciation of beautiful things into the worship of an ideal beauty
and the transformation of the love of particular
persons into the love of God. These mystical
phrases may acquire a new and more human
meaning if we understand, at least in part, how
they first came to be spoken. We shall then not
think of them merely as the reported sayings of
Plato or Plotinus, Porphyry or Proclus; we shall
not learn them by rote, as the unhappy student
learns the enigmas, which, in the histories of
philosophy, represent all that survives of the doctrine of a Thales or a Pythagoras. We shall
have some notion of the ideas that once prompted
such speech.

And we shall be the better able to reconstruct
those conceptions inasmuch as the reflection by
which they are bred has recurred often in the
world — has recurred, very likely, in our own experience. We are often Platonists without knowing it. In some form or other Platonic ideas occur
in all poetry of passion when it is seasoned with
reflection. They are particularly characteristic of
some Italian poets, scattered from the thirteenth
to the sixteenth centuries. These poets had souls
naturally Platonic; even when they had heard
something of Plato they borrowed nothing from
him. They repeated his phrases, when they did

so, merely to throw the authority of an ancient philosopher over the spontaneous suggestions of their own minds. Their Platonism was all their own: it was Christian, mediæval, and chivalrous, both in origin and expression. But it was all the more genuine for being a reincarnation rather than an imitation of the old wisdom.

Nothing, for example, could be a better object-lesson in Platonism than the well-known sentimental history of Dante. There is no essential importance in the question whether Dante could have read anything of Plato or come indirectly under his influence. The Platonism of Dante, is, in any case, quite his own. It is the expression of his inner experience moulded by the chivalry and theology of his time. He tells us the story himself very quaintly in the "Vita Nuova."

At the age of nine he saw, at a wedding-feast in Florence, Beatrice, then a child of seven, who became, forthwith, the mistress of his thoughts. This precocious passion ruled his imagination for life, so that, when he brings to an end the account of the emotions she aroused in him by her life and death, he tells us that he determined to speak no more about her until he should be able to do so more worthily, and to say of her what had never been said of any woman. In the "Divine Comedy," accordingly, where he fulfils this promise, she appears transfigured into a heavenly protectress and guide,

whose gentle womanhood fades into an impersonation of theological wisdom. But this life-
long devotion of Dante to Beatrice was something
purely mental and poetical; he never ventured to
woo; he never once descended or sought to descend
from the sphere of silent and distant adoration;
his tenderness remained always tearful and dreamy,
like that of a supersensitive child.

Yet, while his love of Beatrice was thus constant
and religious, it was by no means exclusive. Dante
took a wife as Beatrice herself had taken a husband;
the temptations of youth, as well as the affection of
married life, seem to have existed beneath this ideal
love, not unrebuked by it, indeed, but certainly not
disturbing it. Should we be surprised at this
species of infidelity? Should we regard it as proof
of the artificiality and hollowness of that so transcendental passion, and smile, as people have done
in the case of Plato himself, at the thin disguise of
philosophy that covers the most vulgar frailties of
human nature? Or, should we say, with others,
that Beatrice is a merely allegorical figure, and the
love she is said to inspire nothing but a symbol for
attachment to wisdom and virtue? These are old
questions, and insoluble by any positive method,
since they cannot be answered by the facts but only
by our interpretation of them. Our solution can
have little historical value, but it will serve to test
our understanding of the metaphysics of feeling.

To guide us in this delicate business we may appeal to a friend of Dante, his fellow-poet Guido Cavalcanti, who will furnish us with another example of this same sort of idealization, and this same sort of inconstancy, expressed in a manner that will repay analysis. Guido Cavalcanti had a Beatrice of his own — something of the kind was then expected of every gentle knight and poet — and Guido's Beatrice was called Giovanna. Dante seems to acknowledge the parity of his friend's passion with his own by coupling the names of the two ladies, Monna Vanna and Monna Bice, in one or two of the sonnets he addresses to Guido. Now it came to pass that Guido, in the fervour of his devotion, at once chivalrous and religious, bethought him of making a pilgrimage to the tomb of Saint James the Apostle, at Compostela in Spain. Upon this journey — a journey beguiled, no doubt, by thoughts of the beautiful Giovanna he had left in Florence — he halted in the city of Toulouse. But at Toulouse, as chance would have it, there lived a lovely lady by the name of Mandetta, with whom it was impossible for the chivalrous pilgrim not to fall in love; for chivalry is nothing but a fine emblazoning of the original manly impulse to fight every man and love every woman. Now in an interesting sonnet Guido describes the conflict of these two affections, or perhaps we should rather say, their union.

> " There is a lady in Toulouse so fair,
>   So young, so gentle, and so chastely gay,
> She doth a true and living likeness bear
>   In her sweet eyes to Love, whom I obey."

The word I have, to avoid confusion, here rendered by "Love" is in the original "la Donna mia," "my Lady"; so that we have our poet falling in love with Mandetta on account of her striking resemblance to Giovanna. Is this inconstancy or only a more delicate and indirect homage? We shall see; for Guido goes on to represent his soul, according to his custom, as a being that dwells and moves about in the chambers of his heart; and speaking still of Mandetta, the lady of Toulouse, he continues: —

> " Within my heart my soul, when she appeared,
>   Was filled with longing and was fain to flee
> Out of my heart to her, yet was afeared
>   To tell the lady who my Love might be.
> She looked upon me with her quiet eyes,
>   And under their sweet ray my bosom burned,
> Cheered by Love's image, that within them lies."

So far we have still the familiar visible in the new and making its power; Mandetta is still nothing but a stimulus to reawaken the memory of Giovanna. But before the end there is trouble. The sting of the present attraction is felt in contrast to the eternal ideal. There is a necessity of sacrifice, and he cries, as the lady turns away her eyes: —

"Alas ! they shot an arrow as she turned,
And with a death-wound from the piercing dart
My soul came sighing back into my heart."

Perhaps this merely means that the lady was disdainful; had she been otherwise the poet might never have written sonnets about her, and surely not sonnets in which her charms were reduced to a Platonic reminiscence of a fairer ideal. But it is this turning away of the face of love, this ephemeral quality of its embodiments, that usually stimulates the imagination to the construction of a super-sensible ideal in which all those evaporated impulses may meet again and rest in an adequate and permanent object. So that while Guido's "death-wound" was perhaps in reality nothing but the rebuff offered him by a prospective mistress, yet the sting of it, in a mind of Platonic habit, served at once to enforce the distinction between the ideal beauty, so full of sweetness and heavenly charm, which had tempted the soul out of his heart on its brief adventure, and the particular and real object against which the soul was dashed, and from which it returned bruised and troubled to its inward solitude.

So the meditative Guido represents his experience: a new planet swam into his ken radiant with every grace and virtue; yet all the magic of that lady lay in her resemblance to the mysterious Giovanna, the double of Beatrice, the ideal

of the poet's imagination. The soul, at first, went
out eagerly to the new love as to an image and
embodiment of the old, but was afraid, and justly,
to mention the ideal in the presence of the reality.
There is always danger in doing that; it breaks
the spell and reduces us again to the old and
patient loyalty to the unseen. The present thing
being so like the ideal we unhesitatingly pursue it:
but we are quickly disappointed, and the soul returns sighing and mortally wounded, as the new
object of passion fades away.

We may now understand somewhat better that
strange combination of loyalty and disloyalty which
we find in Dante. While the object of love is any
particular thing, it excludes all others; but it includes all others as soon as it becomes a general
ideal. All beauties attract by suggesting the ideal
and then fail to satisfy by not fulfilling it. While
Giovanna remained a woman, Guido, as his after
life plainly showed, had no difficulty in forgetting
her and in loving many others with a frank heart;
but when Giovanna had become a name for the absolute ideal, that sovereign mistress could never be
forgotten, and the thought of her subordinated every
particular attachment and called the soul away from
it. Compared with the ideal, every human perfection becomes a shadow and a deceit; every mortal
passion leaves, as Keats has told us,

"A heart high-sorrowful and cloyed,
   A burning forehead and a parching tongue."

Such is the nature of idealization. Like the
Venus of Apelles, in which all known beauties
were combined, the ideal is the union of all we
prize in all creatures; and the mind that has once
felt the irresistible compulsion to create this ideal
and to believe in it has become incapable of unre-
served love of anything else. The absolute is a
jealous god; it is a consuming fire that blasts the
affections upon which it feeds. For this reason
the soul of Guido, in his sonnet, is mortally
wounded by the shaft of that beauty which has
awakened a vehement longing for perfection without being able to satisfy it. All things become to
the worshipper of the ideal so many signs and
symbols of what he seeks; like the votary who,
kneeling now before one image and now before
another, lets his incense float by all with a certain
abstracted impartiality, because his aspiration
mounts through them equally to the invisible God
they alike represent.

Another aspect of the same process is well described by Shakespeare, in whom Italian influences
count for much, when he says to the person he has
chosen as the object of his idealization : —

> " Thy bosom is endearèd with all hearts
>   Which I, by lacking, have supposèd dead,
> And there reigns love and all love's loving parts
>   And all those friends which I thought burièd.
> How many a holy and obsequious tear
>   Hath dear religious love stolen from mine eye

As interest for the dead, which now appear
 But things removed, which hidden in thee lie.
Thou art the grave where buried love doth live
 Hung with the trophies of my lovers gone,
Who all their parts of me to thee did give :
 That due of many now is thine alone.
Their images I loved I view in thee,
And thou, all they, hast all the all of me.''

We need not, then, waste erudition in trying to
prove whether Dante's Beatrice or Guido's Giovanna or any one else who has been the subject
of the greater poetry of love, was a symbol or a
reality. To poets and philosophers real things
are themselves symbols. The child of seven
whom Dante saw at the Florentine feast was, if
you will, a reality. As such she is profoundly
unimportant. To say that Dante loved her then
and ever after is another way of saying that she
was a symbol to him. That is the way with childish loves. Neither the conscious spell of the
senses nor the affinities of taste and character
can then be powerful, but the sense of loneliness
and the vague need of loving may easily conspire
with the innocence of the eyes to fix upon a
single image and to make it the imaginary goal
of all those instincts which as yet do not know
themselves.

When with time these instincts become explicit
and select their respective objects, if the inmost
heart still remains unsatisfied, as it must in all

profound or imaginative natures, the name and memory of that vague early love may well subsist as a symbol for the perfect good yet unattained. It is intelligible that as time goes on that image, grown thus consciously symbolic, should become interchangeable with the abstract method of pursuing perfection — that Beatrice, that is, should become the same as sacred theology. Having recognized that she was to his childish fancy what the ideals of religion were to his mature imagination, Dante intentionally fused the two, as every poet intentionally fuses the general and the particular, the universal and the personal. Beatrice thenceforth appeared, as Plato wished that our loves should, as a manifestation of absolute beauty and as an avenue of divine grace. Dante merely added his Christian humility and tenderness to the insight of the Pagan philosopher.

The tendency to impersonality, we see, is essential to the ideal. It could not fulfil its functions if it retained too many of the traits of any individual. A blind love, an unreasoning passion, is therefore inconsistent with the Platonic spirit, which is favourable rather to abstraction from persons and to admiration of qualities. These may, of course, be found in many individuals. Too much subjection to another personality makes the expression of our own impossible, and the ideal

K

is nothing but a projection of the demands of our imagination. If the imagination is over-powered by too strong a fascination, by the abso-lute dominion of an alien influence, we form no ideal at all. We must master a passion before we can see its meaning.

For this reason, among others, we find so little Platonism in that poet in whom we might have expected to find most — I mean in Petrarch. Pe-trarch is musical, ingenious, learned, and passion-ate, but he is weak. His art is greater than his thought. In the quality of his mind there is nothing truly distinguished. The discipline of his long and hopeless love brings him little wis-dom, little consolation. He is lachrymose and sentimental at the end as at the beginning, and his best dream of heaven, expressed, it is true, in entrancing verse, is only to hold his lady's hand and hear her voice. Sometimes, indeed, he re-peats what he must have read and heard so often, and gives us his version of Plato in half a son-net. Thus, for instance, speaking of his love for Laura, he says in one place: —

> "Hence comes the understanding of love's scope
> That seeking her to perfect good aspires,
> Accounting little what all flesh desires;
> And hence the spirit's happy pinions ope
> In flight impetuous to the heaven's choirs,
> Wherefore I walk already proud in hope."

If we are looking, however, for more direct expressions of the idealism of feeling, of love, and the sense of beauty passing into religion, we shall do well to turn to another Italian, not so great a poet as Petrarch by any means, but a far greater man — to Michael Angelo. Michael Angelo justly regarded himself as essentially a sculptor, and said even of painting that it was not his art; his verses are therefore both laboured and rough. Yet they have been too much neglected, for they breathe the same pathos of strength, the same agony in hope, as his Titanic designs.

Like every Italian of culture in those days, Michael Angelo was in the habit of addressing little pieces to his friends, and of casting his thoughts or his prayers into the mould of a sonnet or a madrigal. Verse has a greater naturalness and a wider range among the Latin peoples than among the English; poetry and prose are less differentiated. In French, Italian, and Spanish, as in Latin itself, elegance and neatness of expression suffice for verse. The reader passes without any sense of incongruity or anti-climax from passion to reflection, from sentiment to satire, from flights of fancy to homely details: the whole has a certain human sincerity and intelligibility which weld it together. As the Latin languages are not composed of two diverse elements, as English is of Latin and German, so the Latin mind does not have two spheres of sentiment, one vulgar and the other sublime. All changes are variations on a single key, which is the key of intelligence. We must not be surprised, therefore, to find now a message to a friend, now an artistic maxim, now a bit of dialectic, and now a confession of sin, taking the form of verse and filling out the fourteen lines of a sonnet. On the contrary, we must look to these familiar compositions for the most genuine evidence of a man's daily thoughts.

We find in Michael Angelo's poems a few recurring ideas, or rather the varied expression of a single half æsthetic, half religious creed. The soul, he tells us in effect, is by nature made for God and for the enjoyment of divine beauty. All true beauty leads to the idea of perfection; the effort toward perfection is the burden of all art, which labours, therefore, with a superhuman and insoluble problem. All love, also, that does not lead to the love of God and merge into that love, is a long and hopeless torment; while the light of love is already the light of heaven, the fire of love is already the fire of hell. These are the thoughts that perpetually recur, varied now with a pathetic reference to the poet's weariness and old age, now with an almost despairing appeal for divine mercy, often with a powerful and rugged description of the pangs of love, and with a pious acceptance of its discipline. The whole is intense, exalted, and tragic, haunted by something of that profound terror, of that magnificent strength, which we admire in the figures of the Sixtine Chapel, those noble agonies of beings greater than any we find in this world.

What, we may ask, is all this tragedy about? What great sorrow, what great love, had Michael Angelo or his giants that they writhe so supernaturally? As those decorative youths are sprinkled over the Sixtine vault, filled, we know not why, with we know not what emotion, so these scraps of verse, these sibylline leaves of Michael Angelo's, give us no reason for their passion. They tell no story; there seems to have been no story to tell. There is something impersonal and elusive about the subject and occasion of these poems. Attempts have been made to attribute them to discreditable passions, as also to a sentimental love for Vittoria Colonna. But the friendship with Vittoria Colonna was an incident of Michael Angelo's mature years; some of the sonnets and madrigals are addressed to her, but we cannot attribute to her influence the passion and sorrow that seem to permeate them all.

Perhaps there is less mystery in this than the curious would have us see in it. Perhaps the love and beauty, however base their primal incarnation, are really, as they think themselves, aspirations

toward the Most High. In the long studies and
weary journeys of the artist, in his mighty inspiration, in his intense love of the structural beauty of
the human body, in his vicissitudes of fortune and
his artistic disappointments, in his exalted piety,
we may see quite enough explanation for the burden
of his soul. It is not necessary to find vulgar
causes for the extraordinary feelings of an extraordinary man. It suffices that life wore this aspect
to him; that the great demands of his spirit so
expressed themselves in the presence of his world.
Here is a madrigal in which the Platonic theory
of beauty is clearly stated : —

"For faithful guide unto my labouring heart
  Beauty was given me at birth,
  To be my glass and lamp in either art.
  Who thinketh otherwise misknows her worth,
  For highest beauty only gives me light
  To carve and paint aright.
  Rash is the thought and vain
  That maketh beauty from the senses grow.
  She lifts to heaven hearts that truly know,
  But eyes grown dim with pain
  From mortal to immortal cannot go
  Nor without grace of God look up again."

And here is a sonnet, called by Mr. Symonds
"the heavenly birth of love and beauty." I bor-
row in part from his translation:—

"My love's life comes not from this heart of mine.
  The love wherewith I love thee hath no heart,

Turned thither whither no fell thoughts incline
And erring human passion leaves no smart.
Love, from God's bosom when our souls did part,
Made me pure eye to see, thee light to shine,
And I must needs, half mortal though thou art,
In spite of sorrow know thee all divine.
As heat in fire, so must eternity
In beauty dwell ; through thee my soul's endeavour
Mounts to the pattern and the source of thee ;
And having found all heaven in thine eyes,
Beneath thy brows my burning spirit flies
There where I loved thee first to dwell for ever."

Something of this kind may also be found in
the verses of Lorenzo de' Medici, who, like Michael
Angelo, was a poet only incidentally, and even
thought it necessary to apologize in a preface for
having written about love. Many of his compositions are, indeed, trival enough, but his pipings
will not seem vain to the severest philosopher
when he finds them leading to strains like the
following, where the thought rises to the purest
sphere of tragedy and of religion : —

" As a lamp, burning through the waning night,
When the oil begins to fail that fed its fire
Flares up, and in its dying waxes bright
And mounts and spreads, the better to expire ;
So in this pilgrimage and earthly flight
The ancient hope is spent that fed desire,
And if there burn within a greater light
' Tis that the vigil's end approacheth nigher.
Hence thy last insult, Fortune, cannot move,
Nor death's inverted torches give alarm ;

> I see the end of wrath and bitter moan.
> My fair Medusa into sculptured stone
> Turns me no more, my Siren cannot charm.
> Heaven draws me up to its supernal love."

From such spontaneous meditation Lorenzo could even pass to verses officially religious; but in them too, beneath the threadbare metaphors of the pious muse and her mystical paradoxes, we may still feel the austerity and firmness of reason. The following stanzas, for instance, taken from his "Laudi Spirituali," assume a sublime meaning if we remember that the essence to which they are addressed, before being a celestial Monarch into whose visible presence any accident might usher us, was a general idea of what is good and an intransitive rational energy, indistinguishable from the truth of things.

> "O let this wretched life within me die
>   That I may live in thee, my life indeed ;
> In thee alone, where dwells eternity,
>   While hungry multitudes death's hunger feed.
> I list within, and hark ! Death's stealthy tread !
> I look to thee, and nothing then is dead.

> "Then eyes may see a light invisible
>   And ears may hear a voice without a sound, —
> A voice and light not harsh, but tempered well,
>   Which the mind wakens when the sense is drowned,
> Till, wrapped within herself, the soul have flown
> To that last good which is her inmost own.

> "When, sweet and beauteous Master, on that day,
>   Reviewing all my loves with aching heart,

I take from each its bitter self away,
The remnant shall be thou, their better part.
This perfect sweetness be his single store
Who seeks the good ; this faileth nevermore.

" A thirst unquenchable is not beguiled
    By draught on draught of any running river
Whose fiery waters feed our pangs for ever,
    But by a living fountain undefiled.
O sacred well, I seek thee and were fain
To drink ; so should I never thirst again."

Having before us these characteristic expressions
of Platonic feeling, as it arose again in a Christian
age, divorced from the accidental setting which
Greek manners had given it, we may be better able
to understand its essence. It is nothing else than
the application to passion of that pursuit of something permanent in a world of change, of something
absolute in a world of relativity, which was the
essence of the Platonic philosophy. If we may
give rein to the imagination in a matter which
without imagination could not be understood at all,
we may fancy Plato trying to comprehend the
power which beauty exerted over his senses by
applying to the objects of love that profound metaphysical distinction which he had learned to make
in his dialectical studies — the distinction between
the appearance to sense and the reality envisaged
by the intellect, between the phenomenon and the
ideal. The whole natural world had come to seem
to him like a world of dreams. In dreams images

succeed one another without other meaning than
that which they derive from our strange power of
recognition — a power which enables us somehow,
among the most incongruous transformations and
surroundings, to find again the objects of our waking life, and to name those absurd and unmannerly
visions by the name of father or mother or by any
other familiar name. As these resemblances to
real things make up all the truth of our dream, and
these recognitions all its meaning, so Plato thought
that all the truth and meaning of earthly things
was the reference they contained to a heavenly
original. This heavenly original we remember and
recognize even among the distortions, disappear-
ances, and multiplications of its earthly copies.

This thought is easily applicable to the affections; indeed, it is not impossible that it was the
natural transcendence of any deep glance into
beauty, and the lessons in disillusion and idealism
given by that natural metaphysician we call love,
that first gave Plato the key to his general system.
There is, at any rate, no sphere in which the super-
sensible is approached with so warm a feeling of
its reality, in which the phenomenon is so transparent and so indifferent a symbol of something
perfect and divine beyond. In love and beauty, if
anywhere, even the common man thinks he has
visitations from a better world, approaches to a
lost happiness; a happiness never tasted by us in

this world, and yet so natural, so expected, that we look for it at every turn of a corner, in every new face; we look for it with so much confidence, with so much depth of expectation, that we never quite overcome our disappointment that it is not found.

And it is not found, — no, never, — in spite of what we may think when we are first in love. Plato knew this well from his experience. He had had successful loves, or what the world calls such, but he could not fancy that these successes were more than provocations, more than hints of what the true good is. To have mistaken them for real happiness would have been to continue to dream. It would have shown as little comprehension of the heart's experience as the idiot shows of the experience of the senses when he is unable to put together impressions of his eyes and hands and to say, "Here is a table; here is a stool." It is by a parallel use of the understanding that we put together the impressions of the heart and the imagination and are able to say, "Here is absolute beauty: here is God." The impressions themselves have no permanence, no intelligible essence. As Plato said, they are never anything fixed but are always either becoming or ceasing to be what we think them. There must be, he tells us, an eternal and clearly definable object of which the visible appearances to us are the manifold semblance; now by one trait now by another the phantom before us lights up that vague and haunting idea, and makes us utter its name with a momentary sense of certitude and attainment.

Just so the individual beauties that charm our attention and enchain the soul have only a transitive existence; they are momentary visions, irrecoverable moods. Their object is unstable; we never can say what it is, it changes so quickly before our eyes. What is it that a mother loves in her child? Perhaps the babe not yet born, or the babe that grew long ago by her suffering and unrecognized care; perhaps the man to be or the youth that has been. What does a man love in a woman? The girl that is yet, perhaps, to be his, or the wife that once chose to give him her whole existence. Where, among all these glimpses, is the true object of love? It flies before us, it tempts us on, only to escape and turn to mock us from a new quarter. And yet nothing can concern us more or be more real to us than this mysterious good, since the pursuit of it gives our lives whatever they have of true earnestness and meaning, and the approach to it whatever they have of joy.

So far is this ideal, Plato would say, from being an illusion, that it is the source of the world, the power that keeps us in existence. But for it, we should be dead. A profound indifference, an initial torpor, would have kept us from ever opening

our eyes, and we should have no world of business
or pleasure, politics or science, to think about at
all. We, and the whole universe, exist only by
the passionate attempt to return to our perfection,
by the radical need of losing ourselves again in
God. That ineffable good is our natural possession; all we honour in this life is but the partial
recovery of our birthright; every delightful thing
is like a rift in the clouds through which we catch
a glimpse of our native heaven. If that heaven
seems so far away and the idea of it so dim and
unreal, it is because we are so far from perfect, so
much immersed in what is alien and destructive to
the soul.

Thus the history of our loves is the record of
our divine conversations, of our intercourse with
heaven. It matters very little whether this history seems to us tragic or not. In one sense, all
mortal loves are tragic because never is the creature we think we possess the true and final object
of our love; this love must ultimately pass beyond
that particular apparition, which is itself continually passing away and shifting all its lines and
colours. As Heraclitus could never bathe twice in
the same river, because its water had flowed away,
so Plato could never look twice at the same face,
for it had become another. But on the other hand
the most unsuccessful passion cannot be a vain
thing. More, perhaps, than if it had found an

apparent satisfaction, it will reveal to us an object of infinite worth, and the flight of the soul, detached by it from the illusions of common life, will be more straight and steady toward the ultimate good.

Such, if we are not mistaken, is the lesson of Plato's experience and also of that of the Italian poets whom we have quoted. Is this experience something normal? Is it the rational outcome of our own lives? That is a question which each man must answer for himself. Our immediate object will have been attained if we have made more intelligible a tendency which is certainly very common among men, and not among the men least worthy of honour. It is the tendency to make our experience of love rational, as scientific thinking is a tendency to make rational our experience of the outer world. The theories of natural science are creations of human reason; they change with the growth of reason, and express the intellectual impulses of each nation and age. Theories about the highest good do the same; only being less applicable in practice, less controllable by experiment, they seldom attain the same distinctness and articulation. But there is nothing authoritative in those constructions of the intellect, nothing coercive except in so far as our own experience and reflection force us to accept them. Natural science is persuasive because it embodies the momentum

of common sense and of the practical arts; it
carries on their spontaneous processes by more
refined but essentially similar methods.   Moral
science is persuasive under the same conditions,
but these conditions are not so generally found
in the minds of men.   Their conscience is often
superstitious and perfunctory; their imagination
is usually either disordered or dull.   There is little
momentum in their lives which the moralist can
rely upon to carry them onward toward rational
ideals.   Deprived of this support his theories fall
to the ground; they must seem, to every man
whose nature cannot elicit them from his own experience, empty verbiage and irrelevant dreams.

Nothing in the world of fact obliges us to agree
with Michael Angelo when he says that eternity
can no more be separated from beauty than heat
from fire.   Beauty is a thing we experience, a
value we feel; but eternity is something problem-
atical.   It might well happen that beauty should
exist for a while in our contemplation and that
eternity should have nothing to do with it or with
us.   It might well happen that our affections, being the natural expression of our instincts in the
family and in the state, should bind us for a while
to the beings with whom life has associated us
— a father, a lover, a child — and that these affections should gradually fade with the decay of our
vitality, declining in the evening of life, and pass-

ing away when we surrender our breath, without
leading us to any single and supreme good, to any
eternal love. If, therefore, the thoughts and consolations we have been rehearsing have sounded
to us extravagant or unnatural, we cannot justify
them by attempting to prove the actual existence
of their objects, by producing the absolute beauty
or by showing where and how we may come face to
face with God. We may well feel that beauty and
love are clear and good enough without any such
additional embodiments. We may take the world
as it is, without feigning another, and study actual
experience without postulating any that is hypo-
thetical. We can welcome beauty for the pleasure
it affords and love for the happiness it brings,
without asking that these things should receive
supernatural extensions.

But we should have studied Plato and his
kindred poets to little purpose if we thought that
by admitting all this we were rejecting more than
the mythical element that was sometimes mixed
with their ideal philosophy. Its essence is not
touched by any acknowledgment of what seems
true or probable in the realm of actual existence.
Nothing is more characteristic of the Platonic
mind than a complete indifference to the continu-
ance of experience and an exclusive interest in its
comprehension. If we wish to understand this
classic attitude of reason, all we need do is to let

reason herself instruct us. We do not need more data, but more mind. If we take the sights and the loves that our mortal limitations have allowed of, and surrender ourselves unreservedly to their natural eloquence; if we say to the spirit that stirs within them, "Be thou me, impetuous one"; if we become, as Michael Angelo says he was, all eyes to see or all heart to feel, then the force of our spiritual vitality, the momentum of our imagination, will carry us beyond ourselves, beyond an interest in our personal existence or eventual emotions, into the presence of a divine beauty and an eternal truth — things impossible to realize in experience, although necessarily envisaged by thought.

As the senses that perceive, in the act of perceiving assert an absolute reality in their object, as the mind that looks before and after believes in the existence of a past and a future which cannot now be experienced, so the imagination and the heart behold, when they are left free to expand and express themselves, an absolute beauty and a perfect love. Intense contemplation disentangles the ideal from the idol of sense, and a purified will rests in it as in the true object of worship. These are the oracles of reason, the prophecies of those profounder spirits who in the world of Nature are obedient unto death because they belong intrinsically to a world where death is

L

impossible, and who can rise continually, by abstraction from personal sensibility, into identity
with the eternal objects of rational life.

Such a religion must elude popular apprehension
until it is translated into myths and cosmological
dogmas.   It is easier for men to fill out the life of
the spirit by supplementing the facts of experience
by other facts for which there is no evidence than
it is for them to master the given facts and turn
them to spiritual uses.   Many can fight for a
doubtful fact when they cannot perform a difficult
idealization.   They trust, as all men must, to what
they can see; they believe in things as their faculties represent things to them.   By the same right,
however, the rationalizer of experience believes in
his visions; he rests, like the meanest of us, in the
present object of his thought.   So long as we live
at all we must trust in something, at least in the
coherence and permanence of the visible world and
in the value of the objects of our own desires.   And
if we live nobly, we are under the same necessity of
believing in noble things.   However unreal, therefore, these Platonic intuitions may seem to those of
us whose interests lie in other quarters, we may
rest assured that these very thoughts would dominate our minds and these eternal companionships
would cheer our desolation, if we had wrestled as
manfully with the same passions and passed through
the transmuting fire of as great a love.

VI

THE ABSENCE OF RELIGION IN SHAKE-SPEARE

WE are accustomed to think of the universality of Shakespeare as not the least of his glories. No other poet has given so many-sided an expression to human nature, or rendered so many passions and moods with such an appropriate variety of style, sentiment, and accent. If, therefore, we were asked to select one monument of human civilization that should survive to some future age, or be trans-ported to another planet to bear witness to the inhabitants there of what we have been upon earth, we should probably choose the works of Shake-speare. In them we recognize the truest portrait and best memorial of man. Yet the archæologists of that future age, or the cosmographers of that other part of the heavens, after conscientious study of our Shakespearian autobiography, would miscon-ceive our life in one important respect. They would hardly understand that man had had a religion.

There are, indeed, numerous exclamations and in

vocations in Shakespeare which we, who have other means of information, know to be evidences of current religious ideas. Shakespeare adopts these, as he adopts the rest of his vocabulary, from the society about him. But he seldom or never gives them their original value. When Iago says "'*sblood*," a commentator might add explanations which should involve the whole philosophy of Christian devotion; but this Christian sentiment is not in Iago's mind, nor in Shakespeare's, any more than the virtues of Heracles and his twelve labours are in the mind of every slave and pander that cries "*hercule*" in the pages of Plautus and Terence. Oaths are the fossils of piety. The geologist recognizes in them the relics of a once active devotion, but they are now only counters and pebbles tossed about in the unconscious play of expression. The lighter and more constant their use, the less their meaning.

Only one degree more inward than this survival of a religious vocabulary in profane speech is the reference we often find in Shakespeare to religious institutions and traditions. There are monks, bishops, and cardinals; there is even mention of saints, although none is ever presented to us in person. The clergy, if they have any wisdom, have an earthly one. Friar Lawrence culls his herbs like a more benevolent Medea; and Cardinal Wolsey flings away ambition with a profoundly

Pagan despair; his robe and his integrity to heaven are cold comfort to him. Juliet goes to shrift to arrange her love affairs, and Ophelia should go to a nunnery to forget hers. Even the chastity of Isabella has little in it that would have been out of place in Iphigenia. The metaphysical Hamlet himself sees a "true ghost," but so far reverts to the positivism that underlies Shakespeare's thinking as to speak soon after of that "undiscovered country from whose bourn no traveller returns."

There are only two or three short passages in the plays, and one sonnet, in which true religious feeling seems to break forth. The most beautiful of these passages is that in " Richard II," which commemorates the death of Mowbray, Duke of Norfolk: —

> "Many a time hath banished Norfolk fought
> For Jesu Christ in glorious Christian field,
> Streaming the ensign of the Christian cross
> Against black Pagans, Turks, and Saracens;
> And, toiled with works of war, retired himself
> To Italy; and there, at Venice, gave
> His body to that pleasant country's earth,
> And his pure soul unto his captain Christ,
> Under whose colours he had fought so long."

This is tender and noble, and full of an indescribable chivalry and pathos, yet even here we find the spirit of war rather than that of religion, and a deeper sense of Italy than of heaven. More un-

mixed is the piety of Henry V after the battle of
Agincourt : —

> "O God, thy arm was here;
> And not to us, but to thy arm alone,
> Ascribe we all ! — When, without stratagem,
> But in plain shock and even play of battle,
> Was ever known so great and little loss,
> On one part and on the other ? — Take it, God,
> For it is none but thine. . . .
> Come, go we in procession to the village,
> And be it death proclaimèd through our host,
> To boast of this, or take that praise from God,
> Which is his only. . . .
>   Do we all holy rites ;
> Let there be sung *Non nobis* and *Te Deum*."

This passage is certainly a true expression of
religious feeling, and just the kind that we might
expect from a dramatist.   Religion appears here
as a manifestation of human nature and as an
expression of human passion.   The passion, however, is not due to Shakespeare's imagination, but
is essentially historical : the poet has simply not
rejected, as he usually does, the religious element
in the situation he reproduces.[1]

---

[1] " And so aboute foure of the clocke in the afternoone, the
Kynge when he saw no apparaunce of enemies, caused the
retreite to be blowen, and gathering his army togither, gave
thankes to almightie god for so happy a victory, causing his
prelates and chapleines to sing this psalm, *In exitu Israell
de Egipto*, and commandyng every man to kneele downe
on the grounde at this verse ; *Non nobis, domine, non nobis,
sed nomini tuo da gloriam.*   Which done, he caused *Te Deum*,

With this dramatic representation of piety we may couple another, of a more intimate kind, from the Sonnets : —

"Poor soul, the centre of my sinful earth,
    Fooled by these rebel powers that thee array,
    Why dost thou pine within and suffer dearth,
    Painting thy outward walls so costly gay ?
    Why so large cost, having so short a lease,
    Dost thou upon thy fading mansion spend ?
    Shall worms, inheritors of this excess,
    Eat up thy charge ?   Is this thy body's end ?
    Then, soul, live thou upon thy servant's loss,
    And let that pine to aggravate thy store ;
    Buy terms divine by selling hours of dross,
    Within be fed, without be rich no more :
    Then shalt thou feed on death, that feeds on men,
    And death once dead, there's no more dying then."

This sonnet contains more than a natural religious emotion inspired by a single event. It contains reflection, and expresses a feeling not merely dramatically proper but rationally just. A mind that habitually ran into such thoughts would be philosophically pious; it would be spiritual. The Sonnets, as a whole, are spiritual; their passion is transmuted into discipline. Their love, which, whatever its nominal object, is hardly anything but love of beauty and youth in general, is made to triumph over time by a metaphysical transforma-

with certain anthems, to be song, giving laud & praise to god, and not boasting of his owne force or any humaine power."
HOLINSHED.

tion of the object into something eternal. At first
this is the beauty of the race renewing itself by
generation, then it is the description of beauty in
the poet's verse, and finally it is the immortal soul
enriched by the contemplation of that beauty. This
noble theme is the more impressively rendered by
being contrasted with another, with a vulgar love
that by its nature refuses to be so transformed and
transmuted. "Two loves," cries the poet, in a line
that gives us the essence of the whole, "Two loves
I have, — of comfort, and despair."

In all this depth of experience, however, there is
still wanting any religious image. The Sonnets are
spiritual, but, with the doubtful exception of the
one quoted above, they are not Christian. And, of
course, a poet of Shakespeare's time could not have
found any other mould than Christianity for his
religion. In our day, with our wide and conscientious historical sympathies, it may be possible for
us to find in other rites and doctrines than those
of our ancestors an expression of some ultimate
truth. But for Shakespeare, in the matter of religion, the choice lay between Christianity and nothing. He chose nothing; he chose to leave his
heroes and himself in the presence of life and of
death with no other philosophy than that which
the profane world can suggest and understand.

This positivism, we need hardly say, was not due
to any grossness or sluggishness in his imagination.

Shakespeare could be idealistic when he dreamed, as he could be spiritual when he reflected. The spectacle of life did not pass before his eyes as a mere phantasmagoria. He seized upon its principles; he became wise. Nothing can exceed the ripeness of his seasoned judgment, or the occasional breadth, sadness, and terseness of his reflection. The author of "Hamlet" could not be without metaphysical aptitude; "Macbeth" could not have been written without a sort of sibylline inspiration, or the Sonnets without something of the Platonic mind. It is all the more remarkable, therefore, that we should have to search through all the works of Shakespeare to find half a dozen passages that have so much as a religious sound, and that even these passages, upon examination, should prove not to be the expression of any deep religious conception. If Shakespeare had been without metaphysical capacity, or without moral maturity, we could have explained his strange insensibility to religion; but as it is, we must marvel at his indifference and ask ourselves what can be the causes of it. For, even if we should not regard the absence of religion as an imperfection in his own thought, we must admit it to be an incompleteness in his portrayal of the thought of others. Positivism may be a virtue in a philosopher, but it is a vice in a dramatist, who has to render those human passions to which the religious imagination has always given a larger meaning and a richer depth.

Those greatest poets by whose side we are accustomed to put Shakespeare did not forego this advantage. They gave us man with his piety and the world with its gods. Homer is the chief repository of the Greek religion, and Dante the faithful interpreter of the Catholic. Nature would have been inconceivable to them without the supernatural, or man without the influence and companionship of the gods. These poets live in a cosmos. In their minds, as in the mind of their age, the fragments of experience have fallen together into a perfect picture, like the bits of glass in a kaleidoscope. Their universe is a total. Reason and imagination have mastered it completely and peopled it. No chaos remains beyond, or, if it does, it is thought of with an involuntary shudder that soon passes into a healthy indifference. They have a theory of human life; they see man in his relations, surrounded by a kindred universe in which he fills his allotted place. He knows the meaning and issue of his life, and does not voyage without a chart.

Shakespeare's world, on the contrary, is only the world of human society. The cosmos eludes him; he does not seem to feel the need of framing that idea. He depicts human life in all its richness and variety, but leaves that life without a setting, and consequently without a meaning. If we asked him to tell us what is the significance of the passion and beauty he had so vividly displayed, and what is the outcome of it all, he could hardly answer in any other words than those he puts into the mouth of Macbeth : —

> " To-morrow, and to-morrow, and to-morrow,
>   Creeps in this petty pace from day to day,
>   To the last syllable of recorded time ;
>   And all our yesterdays have lighted fools
>   The way to dusty death.   Out, out, brief candle!
>   Life's but a walking shadow, a poor player
>   That struts and frets his hour upon the stage
>   And then is heard no more : it is a tale
>   Told by an idiot, full of sound and fury,
>   Signifying nothing."

How differently would Homer or Dante have answered that question! Their tragedy would have been illumined by a sense of the divinity of life and beauty, or by a sense of the sanctity of suffering and death. Their faith had enveloped the world of experience in a world of imagination, in which the ideals of the reason, of the fancy, and of the heart had a natural expression. They had caught in the reality the hint of a lovelier fable, — a fable in which that reality was completed and idealized, and made at once vaster in its extent and more intelligible in its principle. They had, as it were, dramatized the universe, and endowed it with the tragic unities. In contrast with such a luminous philosophy and so well-digested an experience, the silence of Shakespeare and his philosophical incoherence have something in them that is still heathen; something that makes us wonder whether the northern mind, even in him, did not remain morose and barbarous at its inmost core.

But before we allow ourselves such hasty and general inferences, we may well stop to consider whether there is not some simpler answer to our question. An epic poet, we might say, naturally deals with cosmic themes. He needs supernatural machinery because he depicts the movement of human affairs in their generality, as typified in the figures of heroes whose function it is to embody or to overcome elemental forces. Such a poet's world is fabulous, because his inspiration is impersonal. But the dramatist renders the concrete reality of life. He has no need of a superhuman setting for his pictures. Such a setting would destroy the vitality of his creations. His plots should involve only human actors and human motives: the *deus ex machina* has always been regarded as an interloper on his stage. The passions of man are his all-sufficient material; he should weave his whole fabric out of them.

To admit the truth of all this would not, however, solve our problem. The dramatist cannot be expected to put cosmogonies on the boards. Miracle-plays become dramatic only when they become human. But the supernatural world, which the playwright does not bring before the foot-lights, may exist nevertheless in the minds of his characters and of his audience. He may refer to it, appeal to it, and imply it, in the actions and in the sentiments he attributes to his heroes. And if the comparison of Shakespeare with Homer or Dante on the score of religious in-spiration is invalidated by the fact that he is a dramatist while they are epic poets, a comparison may yet be instituted between Shakespeare and other dramatists, from which his singular insensi-bility to religion will as readily appear.

Greek tragedy, as we know, is dominated by the idea of fate. Even when the gods do not appear in person, or where the service or neglect of them is not the moving cause of the whole play, — as it is in the "Bacchæ" and the "Hippolytus" of Euripides, — still the deep conviction of the limits and conditions of human happiness underlies the fable. The will of man fulfils the decrees of Heaven. The hero manifests a higher force than his own, both in success and in failure. The fates guide the willing and drag the unwilling. There is no such fragmentary view of life as we have in our romantic drama, where accidents make the meaningless happiness or unhappiness of a supersensitive adventurer. Life is seen whole, although in miniature. Its boundaries and its

principles are studied more than its incidents.
The human, therefore, everywhere merges with
the divine. Our mortality, being sharply defined
and much insisted upon, draws the attention all
the more to that eternity of Nature and of law
in which it is embosomed. Nor is the fact of
superhuman control left for our reflection to discover; it is emphatically asserted in those oracles
on which so much of the action commonly turns.

When the Greek religion was eclipsed by the
Christian, the ancient way of conceiving the ultra-
human relations of human life became obsolete.
It was no longer possible to speak with sincerity
of the oracles and gods, of Nemesis and ὕβρις.
Yet for a long time it was not possible to speak
in any other terms. The new ideas were without
artistic definition, and literature was paralyzed.
But in the course of ages, when the imagination
had had time and opportunity to develop a Christian art and a Christian philosophy, the dramatic
poets were ready to deal with the new themes.
Only their readiness in this respect surpassed
their ability, at least their ability to please those
who had any memory of the ancient perfection
of the arts.

The miracle-plays were the beginning. Their
crudity was extreme and their levity of the frank-
est; but they had still, like the Greek plays, a religious excuse and a religious background. They

were not without dramatic power, but their offences against taste and their demands upon faith were too great for them to survive the Renaissance. Such plays as the "Polyeucte" of Corneille and the "Devocion de la Cruz" of Calderon, with other Spanish plays that might be mentioned, are examples of Christian dramas by poets of culture; but as a whole we must say that Christianity, while it succeeded in expressing itself in painting and in architecture, failed to express itself in any adequate drama. Where Christianity was strong, the drama either disappeared or became secular; and it has never again dealt with cosmic themes successfully, except in such hands as those of Goethe and Wagner, men who either neglected Christianity altogether or used it only as an incidental ornament, having, as they say, transcended it in their philosophy.

The fact is, that art and reflection have never been able to unite perfectly the two elements of a civilization like ours, that draws its culture from one source and its religion from another. Modern taste has ever been, and still is, largely exotic, largely a revolution in favour of something ancient or foreign. The more cultivated a period has been, the more wholly it has reverted to antiquity for its inspiration. The existence of that completer world has haunted all minds struggling for self-expression, and interfered, perhaps, with the natural development of their genius. The old art which they could not disregard distracted them from the new ideal, and prevented them from embodying this ideal outwardly; while the same ideal, retaining their inward allegiance, made their revivals of ancient forms artificial and incomplete. The strange idea could thus gain admittance that art was not called to deal with everything; that its sphere was the world of polite conventions. The serious and the sacred things of life were to be left unexpressed and inarticulate; while the arts masqueraded in the forms of a Pagan antiquity, to which a triviality was at the same time attributed which in fact it had not possessed. This unfortunate separation of experience and its artistic expression betrayed itself in the inadequacy of what was beautiful and the barbarism of what was sincere.

When such are the usual conditions of artistic creation, we need not wonder that Shakespeare, a poet of the Renaissance, should have confined his representation of life to its secular aspects, and that his readers after him should rather have marvelled at the variety of the things of which he showed an understanding than have taken note of the one thing he overlooked. To omit religion was after all to omit what was not felt to be congenial to a poet's mind. The poet was to trace for us the passionate and romantic embroideries of life; he was to be artful and humane, and above all he was to be delightful. The beauty and charm of things had nothing any longer to do with those painful mysteries and contentions which made the temper of the pious so acrid and sad. In Shakespeare's time and country, to be religious already began to mean to be Puritanical; and in the divorce between the fulness of life on the one hand and the depth and unity of faith on the other, there could be no doubt to which side a man of imaginative instincts would attach himself. A world of passion and beauty without a meaning must seem to him more interesting and worthy than a world of empty principle and dogma, meagre, fanatical, and false. It was beyond the power of synthesis possessed by that age and nation to find a principle of all passion and a religion of all life.

This power of synthesis is indeed so difficult and rare that the attempt to gain it is sometimes condemned as too philosophical, and as tending to embarrass the critical eye and creative imagination with futile theories. We might say, for instance, that the absence of religion in Shakespeare was a sign of his good sense; that a healthy instinct kept his attention within the sublunary world; and that he was in that respect superior to Homer and to Dante. For, while they allowed their wisdom to clothe itself in fanciful forms, he gave us his in its

M

immediate truth, so that he embodied what they
signified.   The supernatural machinery of their
poems was, we might say, an accidental incum-
brance, a traditional means of expression, which
they only half understood, and which made their
representation of life indirect and partly unreal.
Shakespeare, on the other hand, had reached his
poetical majority and independence.   He rendered
human experience no longer through symbols, but
by direct imaginative representation.   What I have
treated as a limitation in him would, then, appear
as the maturity of his strength.

There is always a class of minds in whom the
spectacle of history produces a certain apathy of
reason.   They flatter themselves that they can
escape defeat by not attempting the highest tasks.
We need not here stop to discuss what value as
truth a philosophical synthesis may hope to attain,
nor have we to protest against the æsthetic preference for the sketch and the episode over a reasoned
and unified rendering of life.   Suffice it to say that
the human race hitherto, whenever it has reached a
phase of comparatively high development and freedom, has formed a conception of its place in Nature,
no less than of the contents of its life; and that
this conception has been the occasion of religious
sentiments and practices ; and further, that every
art, whether literary or plastic, has drawn its
favourite themes from this religious sphere.   The

poetic imagination has not commonly stopped short of the philosophical in representing a superhuman environment of man.

Shakespeare, however, is remarkable among the greater poets for being without a philosophy and without a religion. In his drama there is no fixed conception of any forces, natural or moral, dominating and transcending our mortal energies. Whether this characteristic be regarded as a merit or as a defect, its presence cannot be denied. Those who think it wise or possible to refrain from searching for general principles, and are satisfied with the successive empirical appearance of things, without any faith in their rational continuity or completeness, may well see in Shakespeare their natural prophet. For he, too, has been satisfied with the successive description of various passions and events. His world, like the earth before Columbus, extends in an indefinite plane which he is not tempted to explore.

Those of us, however, who believe in circumnavigation, and who think that both human reason and human imagination require a certain totality in our views, and who feel that the most important thing in life is the lesson of it, and its relation to its own ideal, — we can hardly find in Shakespeare all that the highest poet could give. Fulness is not necessarily wholeness, and the most profuse wealth of characterization seems still inadequate as a

picture of experience, if this picture is not somehow seen from above and reduced to a dramatic
unity, — to that unity of meaning that can suffuse
its endless details with something of dignity, simplicity, and peace.   This is the imaginative power
found in several poets we have mentioned, — the
power that gives certain passages in Lucretius also
their sublimity, as it gives sublimity to many
passages in the Bible.

For what is required for theoretic wholeness is
not this or that system but some system. Its value
is not the value of truth, but that of victorious
imagination. Unity of conception is an æsthetic
merit no less than a logical demand. A fine
sense of the dignity and pathos of life cannot be
attained unless we conceive somehow its outcome
and its relations. Without such a conception our
emotions cannot be steadfast and enlightened.
Without it the imagination cannot fulfil its essential function or achieve its supreme success.
Shakespeare himself, had it not been for the time
and place in which he lived, when religion and
imagination blocked rather than helped each other,
would perhaps have allowed more of a cosmic background to appear behind his crowded scenes. If
the Christian in him was not the real man, at least
the Pagan would have spoken frankly. The material forces of Nature, or their vague embodiment
in some northern pantheon, would then have stood

behind his heroes. The various movements of events would have appeared as incidents in a larger drama to which they had at least some symbolic relation. We should have been awed as well as saddened, and purified as well as pleased, by being made to feel the dependence of human accidents upon cosmic forces and their fated evolution. Then we should not have been able to say that Shakespeare was without a religion. For the effort of religion, says Goethe, is to adjust us to the inevitable; each religion in its way strives to bring about this consummation.

VII

THE POETRY OF BARBARISM

I

It is an observation at first sight melancholy but in the end, perhaps, enlightening, that the earliest poets are the most ideal, and that primitive ages furnish the most heroic characters and have the clearest vision of a perfect life. The Homeric times must have been full of ignorance and suffering. In those little barbaric towns, in those camps and farms, in those shipyards, there must have been much insecurity and superstition. That age was singularly poor in all that concerns the convenience of life and the entertainment of the mind with arts and sciences. Yet it had a sense for civilization. That machinery of life which men were beginning to devise appealed to them as poetical; they knew its ultimate justification and studied its incipient processes with delight. The poetry of that simple and ignorant age was, accordingly, the sweetest and sanest that the world has known; the most faultless in taste, and the most even and lofty in inspiration. Without lacking variety and homeliness, it bathed all things human in the golden light of morning; it clothed sorrow in a kind of majesty, instinct with both self-control and heroic frankness. Nowhere else can we find so noble a rendering of human nature, so spontaneous a delight in life, so uncompromising a dedication to beauty, and such a gift of seeing beauty in everything. Homer, the first of poets, was also the best and the most poetical.

From this beginning, if we look down the history of Occidental literature, we see the power of idealization steadily decline. For while it finds here and there, as in Dante, a more spiritual theme and a subtler and riper intellect, it pays for that advantage by a more than equivalent loss in breadth, sanity, and happy vigour. And if ever imagination bursts out with a greater potency, as in Shakespeare (who excels the patriarch of poetry in depth of passion and vividness of characterization, and in those exquisite bubblings of poetry and humour in which English genius is at its best), yet Shakespeare also pays the price by a notable loss in taste, in sustained inspiration, in consecration, and in rationality. There is more or less rubbish in his greatest works. When we come down to our own day we find poets of hardly less natural endowment (for in endowment all ages are perhaps alike) and with vastly richer sources of inspiration; for they have many arts and literatures behind them,

with the spectacle of a varied and agitated society,
a world which is the living microcosm of its own
history and presents in one picture many races,
arts, and religions. Our poets have more wonderful tragedies of the imagination to depict than had
Homer, whose world was innocent of any essential
defeat, or Dante, who believed in the world's defin-
itive redemption. Or, if perhaps their inspiration
is comic, they have the pageant of mediæval manners, with its picturesque artifices and passionate
fancies, and the long comedy of modern social revolutions, so illusory in their aims and so productive
in their aimlessness. They have, moreover, the
new and marvellous conception which natural science has given us of the world and of the conditions of human progress.

With all these lessons of experience behind
them, however, we find our contemporary poets
incapable of any high wisdom, incapable of any
imaginative rendering of human life and its meaning. Our poets are things of shreds and patches;
they give us episodes and studies, a sketch of
this curiosity, a glimpse of that romance; they
have no total vision, no grasp of the whole reality,
and consequently no capacity for a sane and steady
idealization. The comparatively barbarous ages
had a poetry of the ideal; they had visions of
beauty, order, and perfection. This age of material
elaboration has no sense for those things. Its

fancy is retrospective, whimsical, and flickering; its ideals, when it has any, are negative and partial; its moral strength is a blind and miscellaneous vehemence. Its poetry, in a word, is the poetry of barbarism.

This poetry should be viewed in relation to the general moral crisis and imaginative disintegration of which it gives a verbal echo; then we shall avoid the injustice of passing it over as insignificant, no less than the imbecility of hailing it as essentially glorious and successful. We must remember that the imagination of our race has been subject to a double discipline. It has been formed partly in the school of classic literature and polity, and partly in the school of Christian piety. This duality of inspiration, this contradiction between the two accepted methods of rationalizing the world, has been a chief source of that incoherence, that romantic indistinctness and imperfection, which largely characterize the products of the modern arts. A man cannot serve two masters; yet the conditions have not been such as to allow him wholly to despise the one or wholly to obey the other. To be wholly Pagan is impossible after the dissolution of that civilization which had seemed universal, and that empire which had believed itself eternal. To be wholly Christian is impossible for a similar reason, now that the illusion and cohesion of Christian ages is lost, and for the further reason that

Christianity was itself fundamentally eclectic. Before it could succeed and dominate men even for a
time, it was obliged to adjust itself to reality, to
incorporate many elements of Pagan wisdom, and to
accommodate itself to many habits and passions at
variance with its own ideal.

In these latter times, with the prodigious growth
of material life in elaboration and of mental life in
diffusion, there has supervened upon this old dualism a new faith in man's absolute power, a kind
of return to the inexperience and self-assurance
of youth. This new inspiration has made many
minds indifferent to the two traditional disci-
plines ; neither is seriously accepted by them, for
the reason, excellent from their own point of view,
that no discipline whatever is needed. The memory of ancient disillusions has faded with time.
Ignorance of the past has bred contempt for the
lessons which the past might teach. Men prefer
to repeat the old experiment without knowing that
they repeat it.

I say advisedly ignorance of the past, in spite of
the unprecedented historical erudition of our time ;
for life is an art not to be learned by observation,
and the most minute and comprehensive studies do
not teach us what the spirit of man should have
learned by its long living. We study the past as a
dead object, as a ruin, not as an authority and as
an experiment. One reason why history was less

interesting to former ages was that they were less conscious of separation from the past. The perspective of time was less clear because the synthesis of experience was more complete. The mind does not easily discriminate the successive phases of an action in which it is still engaged; it does not arrange in a temporal series the elements of a single perception, but posits them all together as constituting a permanent and real object. Human nature and the life of the world were real and stable objects to the apprehension of our forefathers; the actors changed, but not the characters or the play. Men were then less studious of derivations because they were more conscious of identities. They thought of all reality as in a sense contemporary, and in considering the maxims of a philosopher or the style of a poet, they were not primarily concerned with settling his date and describing his environment. The standard by which they judged was eternal; the environment in which man found himself did not seem to them subject of any essential change.

To us the picturesque element in history is more striking because we feel ourselves the children of our own age only, an age which being itself singular and revolutionary, tends to read its own character into the past, and to regard all other periods as no less fragmentary and effervescent than itself. The changing and the permanent elements are, indeed, everywhere present, and the bias of the observer may emphasize the one or the other as it will: the only question is whether we find the significance of things in their variations or in their similarities.

Now the habit of regarding the past as effete and as merely a stepping-stone to something present or future, is unfavourable to any true apprehension of that element in the past which was vital and which remains eternal. It is a habit of thought that destroys the sense of the moral identity of all ages, by virtue of its very insistence on the mechanical derivation of one age from another. Existences that cause one another exclude one another; each is alien to the rest inasmuch as it is the product of new and different conditions. Ideas that cause nothing unite all things by giving them a common point of reference and a single standard of value.

The classic and the Christian systems were both systems of ideas, attempts to seize the eternal morphology of reality and describe its unchanging constitution. The imagination was summoned thereby to contemplate the highest objects, and the essence of things being thus described, their insignificant variations could retain little importance and the study of these variations might well seem superficial. Mechanical science, the science of causes, was accordingly neglected, while the science of values, with the arts that express these values, was exclusively pursued. The reverse has now occurred and the spirit of life, innocent of any rationalizing discipline and deprived of an authoritative and adequate method of expression, has relapsed into miscellaneous and shallow exuberance. Religion and art have become short-winded. They have forgotten the old maxim that we should copy in order to be copied and remember in order to be remembered. It is true that the multiplicity of these incompetent efforts seems to many a compensation for their ill success, or even a ground for asserting their absolute superiority. Incompetence, when it flatters the passions, can always find a greater incompetence to approve of it. Indeed, some people would have regarded the Tower of Babel as the best academy of eloquence on account of the variety of oratorical methods prevailing there.

It is thus that the imagination of our time has relapsed into barbarism. But discipline of the heart and fancy is always so rare a thing that the neglect of it need not be supposed to involve any very terrible or obvious loss. The triumphs of reason have been few and partial at any time, and perfect works of art are almost unknown. The failure of art and reason, because their principle is ignored, is therefore hardly more conspicuous than it was when their principle, although

perhaps acknowledged, was misunderstood or dis-
obeyed. Indeed, to one who fixes his eye on the
ideal goal, the greatest art often seems the greatest failure, because it alone reminds him of what
it should have been. Trivial stimulations coming
from vulgar objects, on the contrary, by making us
forget altogether the possibility of a deep satisfaction, often succeed in interesting and in winning
applause. The pleasure they give us is so brief
and superficial that the wave of essential disappointment which would ultimately drown it has
not time to rise from the heart.

The poetry of barbarism is not without its charm.
It can play with sense and passion the more readily
and freely in that it does not aspire to subordinate
them to a clear thought or a tenable attitude of the
will. It can impart the transitive emotions which
it expresses; it can find many partial harmonies of
mood and fancy; it can, by virtue of its red-hot
irrationality, utter wilder cries, surrender itself and
us to more absolute passion, and heap up a more indiscriminate wealth of images than belong to poets
of seasoned experience or of heavenly inspiration.
Irrational stimulation may tire us in the end, but
it excites us in the beginning; and how many conventional poets, tender and prolix, have there not
been, who tire us now without ever having excited
anybody ? The power to stimulate is the beginning of greatness, and when the barbarous poet

has genius, as he well may have, he stimulates all
the more powerfully on account of the crudity of
his methods and the recklessness of his emotions.
The defects of such art — lack of distinction, absence of beauty, confusion of ideas, incapacity
permanently to please — will hardly be felt by the
contemporary public, if once its attention is arrested; for no poet is so undisciplined that he
will not find many readers, if he finds readers at
all, less disciplined than himself.

These considerations may perhaps be best enforced by applying them to two writers of great
influence over the present generation who seem to
illustrate them on different planes — Robert Browning and Walt Whitman. They are both analytic
poets — poets who seek to reveal and express the
elemental as opposed to the conventional; but the
dissolution has progressed much farther in Whitman
than in Browning, doubtless because Whitman began at a much lower stage of moral and intellectual organization; for the good will to be radical
was present in both. The elements to which
Browning reduces experience are still passions,
characters, persons; Whitman carries the disintegration further and knows nothing but moods and
particular images. The world of Browning is a
world of history with civilization for its setting
and with the conventional passions for its motive
forces. The world of Whitman is innocent of

these things and contains only far simpler and
more chaotic elements. In him the barbarism is
much more pronounced; it is, indeed, avowed, and
the "barbaric yawp" is sent "over the roofs of
the world" in full consciousness of its inarticulate
character; but in Browning the barbarism is no
less real though disguised by a literary and scientific language, since the passions of civilized life
with which he deals are treated as so many "barbaric yawps," complex indeed in their conditions,
puffings of an intricate engine, but aimless in their
vehemence and mere ebullitions of lustiness in ad-
venturous and profoundly ungoverned souls.

Irrationality on this level is viewed by Browning
with the same satisfaction with which, on a lower
level, it is viewed by Whitman; and the admirers
of each hail it as the secret of a new poetry which
pierces to the quick and awakens the imagination
to a new and genuine vitality. It is in the rebellion against discipline, in the abandonment of
the ideals of classic and Christian tradition, that
this rejuvenation is found. Both poets represent,
therefore, and are admired for representing, what
may be called the poetry of barbarism in the most
accurate and descriptive sense of this word. For
the barbarian is the man who regards his passions
as their own excuse for being; who does not do-
mesticate them either by understanding their cause
or by conceiving their ideal goal. He is the man

who does not know his derivations nor perceive his tendencies, but who merely feels and acts, valuing in his life its force and its filling, but being careless of its purpose and its form. His delight is in abundance and vehemence; his art, like his life, shows an exclusive respect for quantity and splendour of materials. His scorn for what is poorer and weaker than himself is only surpassed by his ignorance of what is higher.

II

WALT WHITMAN

The works of Walt Whitman offer an extreme illustration of this phase of genius, both by their form and by their substance. It was the singularity of his literary form — the challenge it threw to the conventions of verse and of language — that first gave Whitman notoriety: but this notoriety has become fame, because those incapacities and solecisms which glare at us from his pages are only the obverse of a profound inspiration and of a genuine courage. Even the idiosyncrasies of his style have a side which is not mere peversity or affectation; the order of his words, the procession of his images, reproduce the method of a rich, spontaneous, absolutely lazy fancy. In most poets such a natural order is modified by various governing motives — the thought, the metrical form,

N

the echo of other poems in the memory. By Walt
Whitman these conventional influences are reso-
lutely banished. We find the swarms of men and
objects rendered as they might strike the retina in
a sort of waking dream. It is the most sincere
possible confession of the lowest — I mean the
most primitive — type of perception. All ancient
poets are sophisticated in comparison and give
proof of longer intellectual and moral training.
Walt Whitman has gone back to the innocent
style of Adam, when the animals filed before him
one by one and he called each of them by its name.

In fact, the influences to which Walt Whitman
was subject were as favourable as possible to the
imaginary experiment of beginning the world over
again.   Liberalism and transcendentalism both
harboured some illusions on that score; and they
were in the air which our poet breathed. Moreover
he breathed this air in America, where the newness
of the material environment made it easier to
ignore the fatal antiquity of human nature. When
he afterward became aware that there was or had
been a world with a history, he studied that world
with curiosity and spoke of it not without a certain
shrewdness. But he still regarded it as a foreign
world and imagined, as not a few Americans have
done, that his own world was a fresh creation,
not amenable to the same laws as the old. The
difference in the conditions blinded him, in his

merely sensuous apprehension, to the identity of
the principles.

His parents were farmers in central Long Island
and his early years were spent in that district.
The family seems to have been not too prosperous
and somewhat nomadic; Whitman himself drifted
through boyhood without much guidance. We
find him now at school, now helping the labourers
at the farms, now wandering along the beaches of
Long Island, finally at Brooklyn working in an
apparently desultory way as a printer and sometimes as a writer for a local newspaper. He must
have read or heard something, at this early period,
of the English classics; his style often betrays the
deep effect made upon him by the grandiloquence
of the Bible, of Shakespeare, and of Milton. But
his chief interest, if we may trust his account, was
already in his own sensations. The aspects of
Nature, the forms and habits of animals, the sights
of cities, the movement and talk of common people,
were his constant delight. His mind was flooded
with these images, keenly felt and afterward to be
vividly rendered with bold strokes of realism and
imagination.

Many poets have had this faculty to seize the
elementary aspects of things, but none has had
it so exclusively; with Whitman the surface is
absolutely all and the underlying structure is
without interest and almost without existence.

He had had no education and his natural delight in imbibing sensations had not been trained
to the uses of practical or theoretical intelligence.
He basked in the sunshine of perception and
wallowed in the stream of his own sensibility, as
later at Camden in the shallows of his favourite
brook. Even during the civil war, when he heard
the drum-taps so clearly, he could only gaze at the
picturesque and terrible aspects of the struggle,
and linger among the wounded day after day with
a canine devotion; he could not be aroused either
to clear thought or to positive action. So also in
his poems; a multiplicity of images pass before him
and he yields himself to each in turn with absolute
passivity. The world has no inside; it is a phantasmagoria of continuous visions, vivid, impressive,
but monotonous and hard to distinguish in memory,
like the waves of the sea or the decorations of some
barbarous temple, sublime only by the infinite ag-
gregation of parts.

This abundance of detail without organization,
this wealth of perception without intelligence and
of imagination without taste, makes the singularity of Whitman's genius. Full of sympathy and
receptivity, with a wonderful gift of graphic
characterization and an occasional rare grandeur
of diction, he fills us with a sense of the individuality and the universality of what he describes —
it is a drop in itself yet a drop in the ocean.

The absence of any principle of selection or of a sustained style enables him to render aspects of things and of emotion which would have eluded a trained writer. He is, therefore, interesting even where he is grotesque or perverse. He has accomplished, by the sacrifice of almost every other good quality, something never so well done before. He has approached common life without bringing in his mind any higher standard by which to criticise it; he has seen it, not in contrast with an ideal, but as the expression of forces more indeterminate and elementary than itself; and the vulgar, in this cosmic setting, has appeared to him sublime.

There is clearly some analogy between a mass of images without structure and the notion of an absolute democracy. Whitman, inclined by his genius and habits to see life without relief or organization, believed that his inclination in this respect corresponded with the spirit of his age and country, and that Nature and society, at least in the United States, were constituted after the fashion of his own mind. Being the poet of the average man, he wished all men to be specimens of that average, and being the poet of a fluid Nature, he believed that Nature was or should be a formless flux. This personal bias of Whitman's was further encouraged by the actual absence of distinction in his immediate environment. Surrounded by ugly things and common people, he felt himself happy, ecstatic, overflowing with a kind of patriarchal love. He accordingly came to think that there was a spirit of the New World which he embodied, and which was in complete opposition to that of the Old, and that a literature upon novel principles was needed to express and strengthen this American spirit.

Democracy was not to be merely a constitutional device for the better government of given nations, not merely a movement for the material improvement of the lot of the poorer classes. It was to be a social and a moral democracy and to involve an actual equality among all men. Whatever kept them apart and made it impossible for them to be messmates together was to be discarded. The literature of democracy was to ignore all extraordinary gifts of genius or virtue, all distinction drawn even from great passions or romantic adventures. In Whitman's works, in which this new literature is foreshadowed, there is accordingly not a single character nor a single story. His only hero is Myself, the "single separate person," endowed with the primary impulses, with health, and with sensitiveness to the elementary aspects of Nature. The perfect man of the future, the prolific begetter of other perfect men, is to work with his hands, chanting the poems of some future Walt, some ideally democratic bard. Women are to have as nearly as possible the same character as men: the emphasis is to pass from family life and local ties to the friendship of comrades and the general brotherhood of man. Men are to be vigorous, comfortable, sentimental, and irresponsible.

This dream is, of course, unrealized and unrealizable, in America as elsewhere. Undeniably there are in America many suggestions of such a society and such a national character. But the growing complexity and fixity of institutions necessarily tends to obscure these traits of a primitive and crude democracy. What Whitman seized upon as the promise of the future was in reality the survival of the past. He sings the song of pioneers, but it is in the nature of the pioneer that the greater his success the quicker must be his transformation into something different. When Whitman made the initial and amorphous phase of society his ideal, he became the prophet of a lost cause. That cause was lost, not merely when wealth and intelligence began to take shape in the American Commonwealth, but it was lost at the very foundation of the world, when those laws of evolution were established which Whitman, like Rousseau, failed to understand. If we may trust Mr. Herbert Spencer, these laws involve a passage from the homogeneous to the heterogeneous, and a constant progress at once in differentiation and in organization — all, in a word, that Whitman sys-

tematically deprecated or ignored.   He is surely
not the spokesman of the tendencies of his country,
although he describes some aspects of its past and
present condition: nor does he appeal to those whom
he describes, but rather to the *dilettanti* he despises.
He is regarded as representative chiefly by foreign-
ers, who look for some grotesque expression of the
genius of so young and prodigious a people.

Whitman, it is true, loved and comprehended
men; but this love and comprehension had the
same limits as his love and comprehension of
Nature.   He observed truly and responded to his
observation with genuine and pervasive emotion.
A great gregariousness, an innocent tolerance of
moral weakness, a genuine admiration for bodily
health and strength, made him bubble over with
affection for the generic human creature.   Incapable of an ideal passion, he was full of the milk of
human kindness.   Yet, for all his acquaintance
with the ways and thoughts of the common man
of his choice, he did not truly understand him.
For to understand people is to go much deeper
than they go themselves; to penetrate to their
characters and disentangle their inmost ideals.
Whitman's insight into man did not go beyond a
sensuous sympathy; it consisted in a vicarious
satisfaction in their pleasures, and an instinctive
love of their persons.   It never approached a
scientific or imaginative knowledge of their hearts.

Therefore Whitman failed radically in his dearest ambition: he can never be a poet of the people. For the people, like the early races whose poetry was ideal, are natural believers in perfection. They have no doubts about the absolute desirability of wealth and learning and power, none about the worth of pure goodness and pure love. Their chosen poets, if they have any, will be always those who have known how to paint these ideals in lively even if in gaudy colours. Nothing is farther from the common people than the corrupt desire to be primitive. They instinctively look toward a more exalted life, which they imagine to be full of distinction and pleasure, and the idea of that brighter existence fills them with hope or with envy or with humble admiration.

If the people are ever won over to hostility to such ideals, it is only because they are cheated by demagogues who tell them that if all the flowers of civilization were destroyed its fruits would become more abundant. A greater share of happiness, people think, would fall to their lot could they destroy everything beyond their own possible possessions. But they are made thus envious and ignoble only by a deception: what they really desire is an ideal good for themselves which they are told they may secure by depriving others of their preëminence. Their hope is always to enjoy perfect satisfaction themselves;

and therefore a poet who loves the picturesque aspects of labour and vagrancy will hardly be the poet of the poor. He may have described their figure and occupation, in neither of which they are much interested; he will not have read their souls. They will prefer to him any sentimental story-teller, any sensational dramatist, any moralizing poet; for they are hero-worshippers by temperament, and are too wise or too unfortunate to be much enamoured of themselves or of the conditions of their existence.

Fortunately, the political theory that makes Whitman's principle of literary prophecy and criticism does not always inspire his chants, nor is it presented, even in his prose works, quite bare and unadorned. In "Democratic Vistas" we find it clothed with something of the same poetic passion and lighted up with the same flashes of intuition which we admire in the poems. Even there the temperament is finer than the ideas and the poet wiser than the thinker. His ultimate appeal is really to something more primitive and general than any social aspirations, to something more elementary than an ideal of any kind. He speaks to those minds and to those moods in which sensuality is touched with mysticism. When the intellect is in abeyance, when we would "turn and live with the animals, they are so placid and self-contained," when we are weary of conscience and of ambition, and would yield ourselves for a while to the dream of sense, Walt Whitman is a welcome companion. The images he arouses in us, fresh, full of light and health and of a kind of frankness and beauty, are prized all the more at such a time because they are not choice, but drawn perhaps from a hideous and sordid environment. For this circumstance makes them a better means of escape from convention and from that fatigue and despair which lurk not far beneath the surface of conventional life. In casting off with self-assurance and a sense of fresh vitality the distinctions of tradition and reason a man may feel, as he sinks back comfortably to a lower level of sense and instinct, that he is returning to Nature or escaping into the infinite. Mysticism makes us proud and happy to renounce the work of intelligence, both in thought and in life, and persuades us that we become divine by remaining imperfectly human. Walt Whitman gives a new expression to this ancient and multiform tendency. He feels his own cosmic justification and he would lend the sanction of his inspiration to all loafers and holiday-makers. He would be the congenial patron of farmers and factory hands in their crude pleasures and pieties, as Pan was the patron of the shepherds of Arcadia: for he is sure that in spite of his hairiness and animality, the gods will acknowledge him as one of themselves and smile upon him from the serenity of Olympus.

III

ROBERT BROWNING

If we would do justice to Browning's work as a human document, and at the same time perceive its relation to the rational ideals of the imagination and to that poetry which passes into religion, we must keep, as in the case of Whitman, two things in mind. One is the genuineness of the achievement, the sterling quality of the vision and inspiration; these are their own justification when we approach them from below and regard them as manifesting a more direct or impassioned grasp of experience than is given to mildly blatant, convention-ridden minds. The other thing to remember is the short distance to which this comprehension is carried, its failure to approach any finality, or to achieve a recognition even of the traditional ideals of poetry and religion.

In the case of Walt Whitman such a failure will be generally felt; it is obvious that both his music and his philosophy are those of a barbarian, nay, almost of a savage. Accordingly there is need of dwelling rather on the veracity and simple dignity of his thought and art, on their expression of an order of ideas latent in all better experience. But in the case of Browning it is the success that is obvious to most people. Apart from a certain

superficial grotesqueness to which we are soon
accustomed, he easily arouses and engages the
reader by the pithiness of his phrase, the volume
of his passion, the vigour of his moral judgment,
the liveliness of his historical fancy. It is obvious
that we are in the presence of a great writer, of
a great imaginative force, of a master in the expression of emotion. What is perhaps not so obvious, but no less true, is that we are in the presence
of a barbaric genius, of a truncated imagination, of
a thought and an art inchoate and ill-digested, of a
volcanic eruption that tosses itself quite blindly
and ineffectually into the sky.

The points of comparison by which this becomes
clear are perhaps not in every one's mind, although
they are merely the elements of traditional culture,
æsthetic and moral. Yet even without reference to
ultimate ideals, one may notice in Browning many
superficial signs of that deepest of all failures, the
failure in rationality and the indifference to perfection. Such a sign is the turgid style, weighty
without nobility, pointed without naturalness or
precision. Another sign is the "realism" of the
personages, who, quite like men and women in
actual life, are always displaying traits of character and never attaining character as a whole.
Other hints might be found in the structure of
the poems, where the dramatic substance does not
achieve a dramatic form; in the metaphysical dis-

cussion, with its confused prolixity and absence
of result; in the moral ideal, where all energies
figure without their ultimate purposes; in the
religion, which breaks off the expression of this
life in the middle, and finds in that suspense an
argument for immortality. In all this, and much
more that might be recalled, a person coming to
Browning with the habits of a cultivated mind
might see evidence of some profound incapacity in
the poet; but more careful reflection is necessary
to understand the nature of this incapacity, its
cause, and the peculiar accent which its presence
gives to those ideas and impulses which Browning
stimulates in us.

There is the more reason for developing this
criticism (which might seem needlessly hostile and
which time and posterity will doubtless make in
their own quiet and decisive fashion) in that
Browning did not keep within the sphere of
drama and analysis, where he was strong, but
allowed his own temperament and opinions to
vitiate his representation of life, so that he sometimes turned the expression of a violent passion
into the last word of what he thought a religion.
He had a didactic vein, a habit of judging the
spectacle he evoked and of loading the passions he
depicted with his visible sympathy or scorn.

Now a chief support of Browning's popularity is
that he is, for many, an initiator into the deeper

mysteries of passion, a means of escaping from the
moral poverty of their own lives and of feeling the
rhythm and compulsion of the general striving.
He figures, therefore, distinctly as a prophet, as a
bearer of glad tidings, and it is easy for those who
hail him as such to imagine that, knowing the
labour of life so well, he must know something
also of its fruits, and that in giving us the feeling
of existence, he is also giving us its meaning.
There is serious danger that a mind gathering
from his pages the raw materials of truth, the un-
threshed harvest of reality, may take him for a
philosopher, for a rationalizer of what he describes.
Awakening may be mistaken for enlightenment,
and the galvanizing of torpid sensations and impulses for wisdom.

Against such fatuity reason should raise her
voice. The vital and historic forces that produce
illusions of this sort in large groups of men are
indeed beyond the control of criticism. The ideas
of passion are more vivid than those of memory,
until they become memories in turn. They must
be allowed to fight out their desperate battle
against the laws of Nature and reason. But it
is worth while in the meantime, for the sake of the
truth and of a just philosophy, to meet the varying
though perpetual charlatanism of the world with a
steady protest. As soon as Browning is proposed
to us as a leader, as soon as we are asked to be

not the occasional patrons of his art, but the pupils of his philosophy, we have a right to express the radical dissatisfaction which we must feel, if we are rational, with his whole attitude and temper of mind.

The great dramatists have seldom dealt with perfectly virtuous characters. The great poets have seldom represented mythologies that would bear scientific criticism. But by an instinct which constituted their greatness they have cast these mixed materials furnished by life into forms congenial to the specific principles of their art, and by this transformation they have made acceptable in the æsthetic sphere things that in the sphere of reality were evil or imperfect: in a word, their works have been beautiful as works of art. Or, if their genius exceeded that of the technical poet and rose to prophetic intuition, they have known how to create ideal characters, not possessed, perhaps, of every virtue accidentally needed in this world, but possessed of what is ideally better, of internal greatness and perfection. They have also known how to select and reconstruct their mythology so as to make it a true interpretation of moral life. When we read the maxims of Iago, Falstaff, or Hamlet, we are delighted if the thought strikes us as true, but we are not less delighted if it strikes us as false. These characters are not presented to us in order to enlarge our

capacities of passion nor in order to justify themselves as processes of redemption; they are there,
clothed in poetry and imbedded in plot, to entertain
us with their imaginable feelings and their interesting errors. The poet, without being especially a
philosopher, stands by virtue of his superlative
genius on the plane of universal reason, far above
the passionate experience which he overlooks and
on which he reflects; and he raises us for the
moment to his own level, to send us back again, if
not better endowed for practical life, at least not
unacquainted with speculation.

With Browning the case is essentially different.
When his heroes are blinded by passion and warped
by circumstance, as they almost always are, he
does not describe the fact from the vantage-ground
of the intellect and invite us to look at it from that
point of view. On the contrary, his art is all self-
expression or satire. For the most part his hero,
like Whitman's, is himself; not appearing, as in
the case of the American bard, *in puris naturalibus*,
but masked in all sorts of historical and romantic
finery. Sometimes, however, the personage, like
Guido in "The Ring and the Book" or the "frus-
trate ghosts" of other poems, is merely a Marsyas,
shown flayed and quivering to the greater glory
of the poet's ideal Apollo. The impulsive utter-
ances and the crudities of most of the speakers
are passionately adopted by the poet as his own.

o

He thus perverts what might have been a triumph of imagination into a failure of reason.

This circumstance has much to do with the fact that Browning, in spite of his extraordinary gift for expressing emotion, has hardly produced works purely and unconditionally delightful. They not only portray passion, which is interesting, but they betray it, which is odious. His art was still in the service of the will. He had not attained, in studying the beauty of things, that detachment of the phenomenon, that love of the form for its own sake, which is the secret of contemplative satisfaction. Therefore, the lamentable accidents of his personality and opinions, in themselves no worse than those of other mortals, passed into his art. He did not seek to elude them: he had no free speculative faculty to dominate them by. Or, to put the same thing differently, he was too much in earnest in his fictions, he threw himself too unreservedly into his creations. His imagination, like the imagination we have in dreams, was merely a vent for personal preoccupations. His art was inspired by purposes less simple and universal than the ends of imagination itself. His play of mind consequently could not be free or pure. The creative impulse could not reach its goal or manifest in any notable degree its own organic ideal.

We may illustrate these assertions by considering Browning's treatment of the passion of love, a passion to which he gives great prominence and in which he finds the highest significance.

Love is depicted by Browning with truth, with vehemence, and with the constant conviction that it is the supreme thing in life. The great variety of occasions in which it appears in his pages and the different degrees of elaboration it receives, leave it always of the same quality — the quality of passion. It never sinks into sensuality; in spite of its frequent extreme crudeness, it is always, in Browning's hands, a passion of the imagination, it is always love. On the other hand it never rises into contemplation: mingled as it may be with friendship, with religion, or with various forms of natural tenderness, it always remains a passion; it always remains a personal impulse, a hypnotization, with another person for its object or its cause. Kept within these limits it is represented, in a series of powerful sketches, which are for most readers the gems of the Browning gallery, as the last word of experience, the highest phase of human life.

> " The woman yonder, there's no use in life
> But just to obtain her ! Heap earth's woes in one
> And bear them — make a pile of all earth's joys
> And spurn them, as they help or help not this ;
> Only, obtain her ! "

> " When I do come, she will speak not, she will stand,
> Either hand

On my shoulder, give her eyes the first embrace
      Of my face,
Ere we rush, ere we extinguish sight and speech
      Each on each. . . .
O heart, O blood that freezes, blood that burns!
      Earth's returns
For whole centuries of folly, noise, and sin —
      Shut them in —
With their triumphs and their follies and the rest.
      Love is best."

In the piece called " In a Gondola " the lady says
to her lover: —

        " Heart to heart
And lips to lips !   Yet once more, ere we part,
Clasp me and make me thine, as mine thou art."

And he, after being surprised and stabbed in her
arms, replies: —

" It was ordained to be so, sweet ! — and best
Comes now, beneath thine eyes, upon thy breast:
Still kiss me !   Care not for the cowards ; care
Only to put aside thy beauteous hair
My blood will hurt !   The Three I do not scorn
To death, because they never lived, but I
Have lived indeed, and so — (yet one more kiss) —
      can die."

We are not allowed to regard these expressions
as the cries of souls blinded by the agony of passion and lust. Browning unmistakably adopts them
as expressing his own highest intuitions. He so
much admires the strength of this weakness that
he does not admit that it is a weakness at all. It

is with the strut of self-satisfaction, with the sensation, almost, of muscular Christianity, that he boasts of it through the mouth of one of his heroes, who is explaining to his mistress the motive of his faithful services as a minister of the queen: —

> " She thinks there was more cause
> In love of power, high fame, pure loyalty ?
> Perhaps she fancies men wear out their lives
> Chasing such shades. . . .
> I worked because I want you with my soul."

Readers of the fifth chapter of this volume need not be reminded here of the contrast which this method of understanding love offers to that adopted by the real masters of passion and imagination. They began with that crude emotion with which Browning ends; they lived it down, they exalted it by thought, they extracted the pure gold of it in a long purgation of discipline and suffering. The fierce paroxysm which for him is heaven, was for them the proof that heaven cannot be found on earth, that the value of experience is not in experience itself but in the ideals which it reveals. The intense, voluminous emotion, the sudden, overwhelming self-surrender in which he rests was for them the starting-point of a life of rational worship, of an austere and impersonal religion, by which the fire of love, kindled for a moment by the sight of some creature, was put, as it were, into a censer, to burn incense before every image of the

Highest Good. Thus love ceased to be a passion
and became the energy of contemplation: it dif-
fused over the universe, natural and ideal, that
light of tenderness and that faculty of worship
which the passion of love often is first to quicken
in a man's breast.

Of this art, recommended by Plato and practised
in the Christian Church by all adepts of the spiritual life, Browning knew absolutely nothing. About
the object of love he had no misgivings. What
could the object be except somebody or other? The
important thing was to love intensely and to love
often. He remained in the phenomenal sphere:
he was a lover of experience; the ideal did not
exist for him. No conception could be farther
from his thought than the essential conception of
any rational philosophy, namely, that feeling is to
be treated as raw material for thought, and that
the destiny of emotion is to pass into objects which
shall contain all its value while losing all its form-
lessness. This transformation of sense and emotion into objects agreeable to the intellect, into
clear ideas and beautiful things, is the natural work
of reason; when it has been accomplished very imperfectly, or not at all, we have a barbarous mind,
a mind full of chaotic sensations, objectless passions,
and undigested ideas. Such a mind Browning's
was, to a degree remarkable in one with so rich a
heritage of civilization.

The nineteenth century, as we have already said, has nourished the hope of abolishing the past as a force while it studies it as an object; and Browning, with his fondness for a historical stage setting and for the gossip of history, rebelled equally against the Pagan and the Christian discipline. The "Soul" which he trusted in was the barbarous soul, the "Spontaneous Me" of his half-brother Whitman. It was a restless personal impulse, conscious of obscure depths within itself which it fancied to be infinite, and of a certain vague sympathy with wind and cloud and with the universal mutation. It was the soul that might have animated Attila and Alaric when they came down into Italy, a soul not incurious of the tawdriness and corruption of the strange civilization it beheld, but incapable of understanding its original spirit; a soul maintaining in the presence of that noble, unappreciated ruin all its own lordliness and energy, and all its native vulgarity.

Browning, who had not had the education traditional in his own country, used to say that Italy had been his university. But it was a school for which he was ill prepared, and he did not sit under its best teachers. For the superficial ferment, the worldly passions, and the crimes of the Italian Renaissance he had a keen interest and intelligence. But Italy has been always a civilized country, and beneath the trappings and

suits of civilization which at that particular time
it flaunted so gayly, it preserved a civilized heart
to which Browning's insight could never penetrate.
There subsisted in the best minds a trained imagination and a cogent ideal of virtue. Italy had a
religion, and that religion permeated all its life,
and was the background without which even its
secular art and secular passions would not be truly
intelligible. The most commanding and representative, the deepest and most appealing of Italian
natures are permeated with this religious inspiration. A Saint Francis, a Dante, a Michael Angelo,
breathe hardly anything else. Yet for Browning
these men and what they represented may be said
not to have existed. He saw, he studied, and he
painted a decapitated Italy. His vision could not
mount so high as her head.

One of the elements of that higher tradition
which Browning was not prepared to imbibe was
the idealization of love. The passion he represents is lava hot from the crater, in no way moulded,
smelted, or refined. He had no thought of subju-
gating impulses into the harmony of reason. He
did not master life, but was mastered by it. Accordingly the love he describes has no wings; it issues
in nothing. His lovers "extinguish sight and
speech, each on each"; sense, as he says elsewhere,
drowning soul. The man in the gondola may well
boast that he can die; it is the only thing he can

properly do.   Death is the only solution of a love
that is tied to its individual object and inseparable
from the alloy of passion and illusion within itself.
Browning's hero, because he has loved intensely,
says that he has lived; he would be right, if the
significance of life were to be measured by the intensity of the feeling it contained, and if intelligence
were not the highest form of vitality.   But had
that hero known how to love better and had he
had enough spirit to dominate his love, he might
perhaps have been able to carry away the better
part of it and to say that he could not die; for one
half of himself and of his love would have been
dead already and the other half would have been
eternal, having fed —

> "On death, that feeds on men ;
> And death once dead, there's no more dying then."

The irrationality of the passions which Browning
glorifies, making them the crown of life, is so gross
that at times he cannot help perceiving it.

> "How perplexed
> Grows belief !   Well, this cold clay clod
> Was man's heart :
> Crumble it, and what comes next ?   Is it God ? "

Yes, he will tell us.   These passions and follies,
however desperate in themselves and however vain
for the individual, are excellent as parts of the
dispensation of Providence : —

> "Be hate that fruit or love that fruit,
>   It forwards the general deed of man,
>   And each of the many helps to recruit
> The life of the race by a general plan,
>   Each living his own to boot."

If we doubt, then, the value of our own experience, even perhaps of our experience of love, we may appeal to the interdependence of goods and evils in the world to assure ourselves that, in view of its consequences elsewhere, this experience was great and important after all. We need not stop to consider this supposed solution, which bristles with contradictions; it would not satisfy Browning himself, if he did not back it up with something more to his purpose, something nearer to warm and transitive feeling. The compensation for our defeats, the answer to our doubts, is not to be found merely in a proof of the essential necessity and perfection of the universe; that would be cold comfort, especially to so uncontemplative a mind. No: that answer, and compensation are to come very soon and very vividly to every private bosom. There is another life, a series of other lives, for this to happen in. Death will come, and —

> "I shall thereupon
>   Take rest, ere I be gone
> Once more on my adventure brave and new,
>   Fearless and unperplexed,
>   When I wage battle next,
> What weapons to select, what armour to endue."

"For sudden the worst turns the best to the brave,
   The black minute's at end,
And the element's rage, the fiend-voices that rave
   Shall dwindle, shall blend,
Shall change, shall become first a peace out of pain,
   Then a light, then thy breast,
O thou soul of my soul !   I shall clasp thee again
   And with God be the rest ! "

Into this conception of continued life Browning
has put, as a collection of further passages might
easily show, all the items furnished by fancy or tradition which at the moment satisfied his imagination
— new adventures, reunion with friends, and even,
after a severe strain and for a short while, a little
peace and quiet.   The gist of the matter is that we
are to live indefinitely, that all our faults can be
turned to good, all our unfinished business settled,
and that therefore there is time for anything we
like in this world and for all we need in the other.
It is in spirit the direct opposite of the philosophic
maxim of regarding the end, of taking care to leave
a finished life and a perfect character behind us.
It is the opposite, also, of the religious *memento mori*,
of the warning that the time is short before we go
to our account.   According to Browning, there is no
account: we have an infinite credit.   With an
unconscious and characteristic mixture of heathen
instinct with Christian doctrine, he thinks of the
other world as heaven, but of the life to be led
there as of the life of Nature.

Aristotle observes that we do not think the business of life worthy of the gods, to whom we can only attribute contemplation; if Browning had had the idea of perfecting and rationalizing this life rather than of continuing it indefinitely, he would have followed Aristotle and the Church in this matter. But he had no idea of anything eternal; and so he gave, as he would probably have said, a filling to the empty Christian immortality by making every man busy in it about many things. And to the irrational man, to the boy, it is no unpleasant idea to have an infinite number of days to live through, an infinite number of dinners to eat, with an infinity of fresh fights and new love-affairs, and no end of last rides together.

But it is a mere euphemism to call this perpetual vagrancy a development of the soul. A development means the unfolding of a definite nature, the gradual manifestation of a known idea. A series of phases, like the successive leaps of a water-fall, is no development. And Browning has no idea of an intelligible good which the phases of life might approach and with reference to which they might constitute a progress. His notion is simply that the game of life, the exhilaration of action, is inexhaustible. You may set up your tenpins again after you have bowled them over, and you may keep up the sport for ever. The point is to bring them down as often as pos-

sible with a master-stroke and a big bang. That
will tend to invigorate in you that self-confidence
which in this system passes for faith. But it is
unmeaning to call such an exercise heaven, or to
talk of being "with God" in such a life, in any
sense in which we are not with God already and
under all circumstances. Our destiny would rather
be, as Browning himself expresses it in a phrase
which Attila or Alaric might have composed,
"bound dizzily to the wheel of change to slake the
thirst of God."

Such an optimism and such a doctrine of immortality can give no justification to experience which
it does not already have in its detached parts. Indeed, those dogmas are not the basis of Browning's
attitude, not conditions of his satisfaction in
living, but rather overflowings of that satisfaction.
The present life is presumably a fair average of the
whole series of "adventures brave and new" which
fall to each man's share; were it not found delightful in itself, there would be no motive for
imagining and asserting that it is reproduced *in
infinitum*. So too if we did not think that the evil
in experience is actually utilized and visibly swallowed up in its good effects, we should hardly
venture to think that God could have regarded as
a good something which has evil for its condition
and which is for that reason profoundly sad and
equivocal. But Browning's philosophy of life and

habit of imagination do not require the support of
any metaphysical theory. His temperament is perfectly self-sufficient and primary; what doctrines
he has are suggested by it and are too loose to give
it more than a hesitant expression; they are quite
powerless to give it any justification which it
might lack on its face.

It is the temperament, then, that speaks; we
may brush aside as unsubstantial, and even as dis-
torting, the web of arguments and theories which
it has spun out of itself. And what does the
temperament say? That life is an adventure, not
a discipline; that the exercise of energy is the
absolute good, irrespective of motives or of consequences. These are the maxims of a frank barbarism; nothing could express better the lust of
life, the dogged unwillingness to learn from experience, the contempt for rationality, the carelessness
about perfection, the admiration for mere force, in
which barbarism always betrays itself. The vague
religion which seeks to justify this attitude is really
only another outburst of the same irrational impulse.

In Browning this religion takes the name of
Christianity, and identifies itself with one or two
Christian ideas arbitrarily selected; but at heart it
has far more affinity to the worship of Thor or of
Odin than to the religion of the Cross. The zest
of life becomes a cosmic emotion; we lump the
whole together and cry, " Hurrah for the Uni-

verse!" A faith which is thus a pure matter of lustiness and inebriation rises and falls, attracts or repels, with the ebb and flow of the mood from which it springs. It is invincible because unseizable; it is as safe from refutation as it is rebellious to embodiment. But it cannot enlighten or correct the passions on which it feeds. Like a servile priest, it flatters them in the name of Heaven. It cloaks irrationality in sanctimony; and its admiration for every bluff folly, being thus justified by a theory, becomes a positive fanaticism, eager to defend any wayward impulse.

Such barbarism of temper and thought could hardly, in a man of Browning's independence and spontaneity, be without its counterpart in his art. When a man's personal religion is passive, as Shakespeare's seems to have been, and is adopted without question or particular interest from the society around him, we may not observe any analogy between it and the free creations of that man's mind. Not so when the religion is created afresh by the private imagination; it is then merely one among many personal works of art, and will naturally bear a family likeness to the others. The same individual temperament, with its limitations and its bias, will appear in the art which has appeared in the religion. And such is the case with Browning. His limitations as a poet are the counterpart of his limitations as a

moralist and theologian; only in the poet they
are not so regrettable. Philosophy and religion
are nothing if not ultimate; it is their business
to deal with general principles and final aims.
Now it is in the conception of things fundamental
and ultimate that Browning is weak; he is strong
in the conception of things immediate. The pulse
of the emotion, the bobbing up of the thought, the
streaming of the reverie — these he can note down
with picturesque force or imagine with admirable
fecundity.

Yet the limits of such excellence are narrow,
for no man can safely go far without the guidance
of reason. His long poems have no structure
— for that name cannot be given to the singular mechanical division of " The Ring and the
Book." Even his short poems have no completeness, no limpidity. They are little torsos made
broken so as to stimulate the reader to the restoration of their missing legs and arms. What is
admirable in them is pregnancy of phrase, vividness of passion and sentiment, heaped-up scraps
of observation, occasional flashes of light, occasional beauties of versification, — all like

> " the quick sharp scratch
> And blue spurt of a lighted match."

There is never anything largely composed in the
spirit of pure beauty, nothing devotedly finished,

nothing simple and truly just. The poet's mind cannot reach equilibrium; at best he oscillates between opposed extravagances; his final word is still a *boutade*, still an explosion. He has no sustained nobility of style. He affects with the reader a confidential and vulgar manner, so as to be more sincere and to feel more at home. Even in the poems where the effort at impersonality is most successful, the dramatic disguise is usually thrown off in a preface, epilogue or parenthesis. The author likes to remind us of himself by some confidential wink or genial poke in the ribs, by some little interlarded sneer. We get in these tricks of manner a taste of that essential vulgarity, that indifference to purity and distinction, which is latent but pervasive in all the products of this mind. The same disdain of perfection which appears in his ethics appears here in his verse, and impairs its beauty by allowing it to remain too often obscure, affected, and grotesque.

Such a correspondence is natural: for the same powers of conception and expression are needed in fiction, which, if turned to reflection, would produce a good philosophy. Reason is necessary to the perception of high beauty. Discipline is indispensable to art. Work from which these qualities are absent must be barbaric; it can have no ideal form and must appeal to us only through the sensuousness and profusion of its materials.

P

We are invited by it to lapse into a miscellaneous appreciativeness, into a subservience to every
detached impression. And yet, if we would only
reflect even on these disordered beauties, we should
see that the principle by which they delight us
is a principle by which an ideal, an image of perfection, is inevitably evoked. We can have no
pleasure or pain, nor any preference whatsoever,
without implicitly setting up a standard of excellence, an ideal of what would satisfy us there. To
make these implicit ideals explicit, to catch their
hint, to work out their theme, and express clearly
to ourselves and to the world what they are demanding in the place of the actual — that is the
labour of reason and the task of genius. The two
cannot be divided. Clarification of ideas and dis-
entanglement of values are as essential to æsthetic
activity as to intelligence. A failure of reason is
a failure of art and taste.

The limits of Browning's art, like the limits of
Whitman's, can therefore be understood by considering his mental habit. Both poets had powerful
imaginations, but the type of their imaginations
was low. In Whitman imagination was limited to
marshalling sensations in single file; the embroideries he made around that central line were simple
and insignificant. His energy was concentrated
on that somewhat animal form of contemplation,
of which, for the rest, he was a great, perhaps an

unequalled master.   Browning rose above that
level; with him sensation is usually in the background; he is not particularly a poet of the senses
or of ocular vision.   His favourite subject-matter
is rather the stream of thought and feeling in
the mind; he is the poet of soliloquy.   Nature
and life as they really are, rather than as they
may appear to the ignorant and passionate partici-
pant in them, lie beyond his range.   Even in his
best dramas, like "A Blot in the 'Scutcheon" or
"Colombe's Birthday," the interest remains in the
experience of the several persons as they explain
it to us.   The same is the case in "The Ring and
the Book," the conception of which, in twelve
monstrous soliloquies, is a striking evidence of the
poet's predilection for this form.

The method is, to penetrate by sympathy rather
than to portray by intelligence.   The most authoritative insight is not the poet's or the spectator's,
aroused and enlightened by the spectacle, but the
various heroes' own, in their moment of intensest
passion.   We therefore miss the tragic relief and
exaltation, and come away instead with the uncom-
fortable feeling that an obstinate folly is apparently the most glorious and choiceworthy thing in
the world.   This is evidently the poet's own illusion,
and those who do not happen to share it must feel
that if life were really as irrational as he thinks
it, it would be not only profoundly discouraging,

which it often is, but profoundly disgusting, which
it surely is not; for at least it reveals the ideal
which it fails to attain.

This ideal Browning never disentangles. For
him the crude experience is the only end, the
endless struggle the only ideal, and the perturbed
"Soul" the only organon of truth. The arrest
of his intelligence at this point, before it has
envisaged any rational object, explains the arrest
of his dramatic art at soliloquy. His immersion
in the forms of self-consciousness prevents him
from dramatizing the real relations of men and
their thinkings to one another, to Nature, and to
destiny. For in order to do so he would have
had to view his characters from above (as Cer-
vantes did, for instance), and to see them not
merely as they appeared to themselves, but as
they appear to reason. This higher attitude, however, was not only beyond Browning's scope, it was
positively contrary to his inspiration. Had he
reached it, he would no longer have seen the universe through the "Soul," but through the intellect, and he would not have been able to cry, "How
the world is made for each one of us!" On the
contrary, the "Soul" would have figured only in
its true conditions, in all its ignorance and dependence, and also in its essential teachableness, a point
against which Browning's barbaric wilfulness particularly rebelled. Rooted in his persuasion that

the soul is essentially omnipotent and that to live hard can never be to live wrong, he remained fascinated by the march and method of self-consciousness, and never allowed himself to be weaned from that romantic fatuity by the energy of rational imagination, which prompts us not to regard our ideas as mere filling of a dream, but rather to build on them the conception of permanent objects and overruling principles, such as Nature, society, and the other ideals of reason. A full-grown imagination deals with these things, which do not obey the laws of psychological progression, and cannot be described by the methods of soliloquy.

We thus see that Browning's sphere, though more subtle and complex than Whitman's, was still elementary. It lay far below the spheres of social and historical reality in which Shakespeare moved; far below the comprehensive and cosmic sphere of every great epic poet. Browning did not even reach the intellectual plane of such contemporary poets as Tennyson and Matthew Arnold, who, whatever may be thought of their powers, did not study consciousness for itself, but for the sake of its meaning and of the objects which it revealed. The best things that come into a man's consciousness are the things that take him out of it — the rational things that are independent of his personal perception and of his personal existence. These he approaches with his reason, and they, in the same measure, endow him with their immortality. But precisely these things — the objects of science and of the constructive imagination — Browning always saw askance, in the outskirts of his field of vision, for his eye was fixed and riveted on the soliloquizing Soul. And this Soul being, to his apprehension, irrational, did not give itself over to those permanent objects which might otherwise have occupied it, but ruminated on its own accidental emotions, on its love-affairs, and on its hopes of going on so ruminating for ever.

The pathology of the human mind — for the normal, too, is pathological when it is not referred to the ideal — the pathology of the human mind is a very interesting subject, demanding great gifts and great ingenuity in its treatment. Browning ministers to this interest, and possesses this ingenuity and these gifts. More than any other poet he keeps a kind of speculation alive in the now large body of sentimental, eager-minded people, who no longer can find in a definite religion a form and language for their imaginative life. That this service is greatly appreciated speaks well for the ineradicable tendency in man to study himself and his destiny. We do not deny the achievement when we point out its nature and limitations. It does not cease to be something because it is taken to be more than it is.

In every imaginative sphere the nineteenth century has been an era of chaos, as it has been an era of order and growing organization in the spheres of science and of industry.   An ancient doctrine of the philosophers asserts that to chaos the world must ultimately return.   And what is perhaps true of the cycles of cosmic change is certainly true of the revolutions of culture.   Nothing lasts for ever: languages, arts, and religions disintegrate with time. Yet the perfecting of such forms is the only criterion of progress; the destruction of them the chief evidence of decay.   Perhaps fate intends that we should have, in our imaginative decadence, the consolation of fancying that we are still progressing, and that the disintegration of religion and the arts is bringing us nearer to the protoplasm of sensation and passion.   If energy and actuality are all that we care for, chaos is as good as order, and barbarism as good as discipline — better, perhaps, since impulse is not then restrained within any bounds of reason or beauty.   But if the powers of the human mind are at any time adequate to the task of digesting experience, clearness and order inevitably supervene.   The moulds of thought are imposed upon Nature, and the conviction of a definite truth arises together with the vision of a supreme perfection.   It is only at such periods that the human animal vindicates his title of rational.   If such an epoch should return, people will no doubt retrace our present gropings with interest and see in them gradual approaches to their own achievement. Whitman and Browning might well figure then as representatives of our time. For the merit of being representative cannot be denied them. The mind of our age, like theirs, is choked with materials, emotional, and inconclusive. They merely aggravate our characteristics, and their success with us is due partly to their own absolute strength and partly to our common weakness. If once, however, this imaginative weakness could be overcome, and a form found for the crude matter of experience, men might look back from the height of a new religion and a new poetry upon the present troubles of the spirit; and perhaps even these things might then be pleasant to remember.

VIII

EMERSON

THOSE who knew Emerson, or who stood so near
to his time and to his circle that they caught some
echo of his personal influence, did not judge him
merely as a poet or philosopher, nor identify his
efficacy with that of his writings. His friends and
neighbours, the congregations he preached to in his
younger days, the audiences that afterward listened to his lectures, all agreed in a veneration
for his person which had nothing to do with their
understanding or acceptance of his opinions. They
flocked to him and listened to his word, not so
much for the sake of its absolute meaning as for
the atmosphere of candour, purity, and serenity
that hung about it, as about a sort of sacred music.
They felt themselves in the presence of a rare and
beautiful spirit, who was in communion with a
higher world. More than the truth his teaching
might express, they valued the sense it gave them
of a truth that was inexpressible. They became
aware, if we may say so, of the ultra-violet rays of
his spectrum, of the inaudible highest notes of his
gamut, too pure and thin for common ears.

This effect was by no means due to the possession
on the part of Emerson of the secret of the universe, or even of a definite conception of ultimate
truth.   He was not a prophet who had once for all
climbed his Sinai or his Tabor, and having there
beheld the transfigured reality, descended again to
make authoritative report of it to the world.   Far
from it.   At bottom he had no doctrine at all.
The deeper he went and the more he tried to
grapple with fundamental conceptions, the vaguer
and more elusive they became in his hands.   Did
he know what he meant by Spirit or the " Over-
Soul " ?   Could he say what he understood by the
terms, so constantly on his lips, Nature, Law, God,
Benefit, or Beauty ?   He could not, and the consciousness of that incapacity was so lively within
him that he never attempted to give articulation to
his philosophy.   His finer instinct kept him from
doing that violence to his inspiration.

The source of his power lay not in his doctrine,
but in his temperament, and the rare quality of his
wisdom was due less to his reason than to his imagination.   Reality eluded him ; he had neither dili-
gence nor constancy enough to master and possess
it ; but his mind was open to all philosophic influences, from whatever quarter they might blow; the
lessons of science and the hints of poetry worked
themselves out in him to a free and personal religion.   He differed from the plodding many, not in

knowing things better, but in having more ways of knowing them. His grasp was not particularly firm, he was far from being, like a Plato or an Aristotle, past master in the art and the science of life. But his mind was endowed with unusual plasticity, with unusual spontaneity and liberty of movement — it was a fairyland of thoughts and fancies. He was like a young god making experiments in creation: he blotched the work, and always began again on a new and better plan. Every day he said, "Let there be light," and every day the light was new. His sun, like that of Heraclitus, was different every morning.

What seemed, then, to the more earnest and less critical of his hearers a revelation from above was in truth rather an insurrection from beneath, a shaking loose from convention, a disintegration of the normal categories of reason in favour of various imaginative principles, on which the world might have been built, if it had been built differently. This gift of revolutionary thinking allowed new aspects, hints of wider laws, premonitions of unthought-of fundamental unities to spring constantly into view. But such visions were necessarily fleeting, because the human mind had long before settled its grammar, and discovered, after much groping and many defeats, the general forms in which experience will allow itself to be stated. These general forms are the principles of common sense and positive science, no less imaginative in their origin than those notions which we now call transcendental, but grown prosaic, like the metaphors of common speech, by dint of repetition.

Yet authority, even of this rational kind, sat lightly upon Emerson. To reject tradition and think as one might have thought if no man had ever existed before was indeed the aspiration of the Transcendentalists, and although Emerson hardly regarded himself as a member of that school, he largely shared its tendency and passed for its spokesman. Without protesting against tradition, he smilingly eluded it in his thoughts, untamable in their quiet irresponsibility. He fled to his woods or to his "pleachèd garden," to be the creator of his own worlds in solitude and freedom. No wonder that he brought thence to the tightly conventional minds of his contemporaries a breath as if from paradise. His simplicity in novelty, his profundity, his ingenuous ardour must have seemed to them something heavenly, and they may be excused if they thought they detected inspiration even in his occasional thin paradoxes and guileless whims. They were stifled with conscience and he brought them a breath of Nature; they were surfeited with shallow controversies and he gave them poetic truth.

Imagination, indeed, is his single theme. As a preacher might under every text enforce the same lessons of the gospel, so Emerson traces in every sphere the same spiritual laws of experience — compensation, continuity, the self-expression of the Soul in the forms of Nature and of society, until she finally recognizes herself in her own work and sees its beneficence and beauty. His constant refrain is the omnipotence of imaginative thought; its power first to make the world, then to understand it, and finally to rise above it. All Nature is an embodiment of our native fancy, all history a drama in which the innate possibilities of the spirit are enacted and realized. While the conflict of life and the shocks of experience seem to bring us face to face with an alien and overwhelming power, reflection can humanize and rationalize that power by conceiving its laws; and with this recognition of the rationality of all things comes the sense of their beauty and order. The destruction which Nature seems to prepare for our special hopes is thus seen to be the victory of our impersonal interests. To awaken in us this spiritual insight, an elevation of mind which is at once an act of comprehension and of worship, to substitute it for lower passions and more servile forms of intelligence — that is Emerson's constant effort. All his resources of illustration, observation, and rhetoric are used to deepen and clarify this sort of wisdom.

Such thought is essentially the same that is

found in the German romantic or idealistic philosophers, with whom Emerson's affinity is remarkable, all the more as he seems to have borrowed little or nothing from their works. The critics of human nature, in the eighteenth century, had shown how much men's ideas depend on their predispositions, on the character of their senses and the habits of their intelligence. Seizing upon this thought and exaggerating it, the romantic philosophers attributed to the spirit of man the omnipotence which had belonged to God, and felt that in this way they were reasserting the supremacy of mind over matter and establishing it upon a safe and rational basis.

The Germans were great system-makers, and Emerson cannot rival them in the sustained effort of thought by which they sought to reinterpret every sphere of being according to their chosen principles. But he surpassed them in an instinctive sense of what he was doing. He never represented his poetry as science, nor countenanced the formation of a new sect that should nurse the sense of a private and mysterious illumination, and relight the fagots of passion and prejudice. He never tried to seek out and defend the universal implications of his ideas, and never wrote the book he had once planned on the law of compensation, foreseeing, we may well believe, the sophistries in which he would have been directly involved. He fortunately preferred a fresh statement on a fresh subject. A suggestion once given, the spirit once aroused to speculation, a glimpse once gained of some ideal harmony, he chose to descend again to common sense and to touch the earth for a moment before another flight. The faculty of idealization was itself what he valued. Philosophy for him was rather a moral energy flowering into sprightliness of thought than a body of serious and defensible doctrines. In practising transcendental speculation only in this poetic and sporadic fashion, Emerson retained its true value and avoided its greatest danger. He secured the freedom and fertility of his thought and did not allow one conception of law or one hint of harmony to sterilize the mind and prevent the subsequent birth within it of other ideas, no less just and imposing than their predecessors. For we are not dealing at all in such a philosophy with matters of fact or with such verifiable truths as exclude their opposites. We are dealing only with imagination, with the art of conception, and with the various forms in which reflection, like a poet, may compose and recompose human experience.

A certain disquiet mingled, however, in the minds of Emerson's contemporaries with the admiration they felt for his purity and genius. They saw that he had forsaken the doctrines of the Church; and they were not sure whether he held quite unequivocally

any doctrine whatever.   We may not all of us share
the concern for orthodoxy which usually caused
this puzzled alarm : we may understand that it was
not Emerson's vocation to be definite and dogmatic
in religion any more than in philosophy.   Yet that
disquiet will not, even for us, wholly disappear.
It is produced by a defect which naturally accompanies imagination in all but the greatest minds.
I mean disorganization.   Emerson not only conceived things in new ways, but he seemed to think
the new ways might cancel and supersede the old.
His imagination was to invalidate the understanding.   That inspiration which should come to fulfil
seemed too often to come to destroy.   If he was able
so constantly to stimulate us to fresh thoughts, was
it not because he demolished the labour of long
ages of reflection ?   Was not the startling effect of
much of his writing due to its contradiction to tradition and to common sense ?

So long as he is a poet and in the enjoyment of
his poetic license, we can blame this play of mind
only by a misunderstanding.   It is possible to
think otherwise than as common sense thinks ;
there are other categories beside those of science.
When we employ them we enlarge our lives.   We
add to the world of fact any number of worlds of
the imagination in which human nature and the
eternal relations of ideas may be nobly expressed.
So far our imaginative fertility is only a benefit :

it surrounds us with the congenial and necessary
radiation of art and religion.   It manifests our
moral vitality in the bosom of Nature.

But sometimes imagination invades the sphere of
understanding and seems to discredit its indispensable work.   Common sense, we are allowed to infer,
is a shallow affair: true insight changes all that.
When so applied, poetic activity is not an unmixed
good.   It loosens our hold on fact and confuses our
intelligence, so that we forget that intelligence has
itself every prerogative of imagination, and has
besides the sanction of practical validity.   We
are made to believe that since the understanding
is something human and conditioned, something
which might have been different, as the senses
might have been different, and which we may yet,
so to speak, get behind — therefore the understanding ought to be abandoned.   We long for higher
faculties, neglecting those we have, we yearn for
intuition, closing our eyes upon experience.   We
become mystical.

Mysticism, as we have said, is the surrender of a
category of thought because we divine its relativity.
As every new category, however, must share this
reproach, the mystic is obliged in the end to give
them all up, the poetic and moral categories no
less than the physical, so that the end of his
purification is the atrophy of his whole nature,
the emptying of his whole heart and mind to make

Q

room, as he thinks, for God. By attacking the authority of the understanding as the organon of knowledge, by substituting itself for it as the herald of a deeper truth, the imagination thus prepares its own destruction. For if the understanding is rejected because it cannot grasp the absolute, the imagination and all its works — art, dogma, worship — must presently be rejected for the same reason. Common sense and poetry must both go by the board, and conscience must follow after: for all these are human and relative. Mysticism will be satisfied only with the absolute, and as the absolute, by its very definition, is not representable by any specific faculty, it must be approached through the abandonment of all. The lights of life must be extinguished that the light of the absolute may shine, and the possession of everything in general must be secured by the surrender of everything in particular.

The same diffidence, however, the same constant renewal of sincerity which kept Emerson's flights of imagination near to experience, kept his mysticism also within bounds. A certain mystical tendency is pervasive with him, but there are only one or two subjects on which he dwells with enough constancy and energy of attention to make his mystical treatment of them pronounced. One of these is the question of the unity of all minds in the single soul of the universe, which is the same in all creatures; another is the question of evil and of its evaporation in the universal harmony of things. Both these ideas suggest themselves at certain turns in every man's experience, and might receive a rational formulation. But they are intricate subjects, obscured by many emotional prejudices, so that the labour, impartiality, and precision which would be needed to elucidate them are to be looked for in scholastic rather than in inspired thinkers, and in Emerson least of all. Before these problems he is alternately ingenuous and rhapsodical, and in both moods equally helpless. Individuals no doubt exist, he says to himself. But, ah! Napoleon is in every schoolboy. In every squatter in the western prairies we shall find an owner—

"Of Caesar's hand and Plato's brain,
   Of Lord Christ's heart, and Shakespeare's strain."

But how? we may ask. Potentially? Is it because any mind, were it given the right body and the right experience, were it made over, in a word, into another mind, would resemble that other mind to the point of identity? Or is it that our souls are already so largely similar that we are subject to many kindred promptings and share many ideals unrealizable in our particular circumstances? But then we should simply be saying that if what makes men different were removed, men would be indistinguishable, or that, in so far as they are now alike, they can understand one another by summoning up their respective experiences in the fancy. There would be no mysticism in that, but at the same time, alas, no eloquence, no paradox, and, if we must say the word, no nonsense.

On the question of evil, Emerson's position is of the same kind. There is evil, of course, he tells us. Experience is sad. There is a crack in everything that God has made. But, ah! the laws of the universe are sacred and beneficent. Without them nothing good could arise. All things, then, are in their right places and the universe is perfect above our querulous tears. Perfect? we may ask. But perfect from what point of view, in reference to what ideal? To its own? To that of a man who renouncing himself and all naturally dear to him, ignoring the injustice, suffering, and impotence in the world, allows his will and his conscience to be hypnotized by the spectacle of a necessary evolution, and lulled into cruelty by the pomp and music of a tragic show? In that case the evil is not explained, it is forgotten; it is not cured, but condoned. We have surrendered the category of the better and the worse, the deepest foundation of life and reason; we have become mystics on the one subject on which, above all others, we ought to be men.

Two forces may be said to have carried Emerson in this mystical direction; one, that freedom of his imagination which we have already noted, and which kept him from the fear of self-contradiction; the other the habit of worship inherited from his clerical ancestors and enforced by his religious education. The spirit of conformity, the unction, the loyalty even unto death inspired by the religion of Jehovah, were dispositions acquired by too long a discipline and rooted in too many forms of speech, of thought, and of worship for a man like Emerson, who had felt their full force, ever to be able to lose them. The evolutions of his abstract opinions left that habit unchanged. Unless we keep this circumstance in mind, we shall not be able to understand the kind of elation and sacred joy, so characteristic of his eloquence, with which he propounds laws of Nature and aspects of experience which, viewed in themselves, afford but an equivocal support to moral enthusiasm. An optimism so persistent and unclouded as his will seem at variance with the description he himself gives of human life, a description coloured by a poetic idealism, but hardly by an optimistic bias.

We must remember, therefore, that this optimism is a pious tradition, originally justified by the belief in a personal God and in a providential government of affairs for the ultimate and positive good of the elect, and that the habit of worship survived in Emerson as an instinct after those positive beliefs had faded into a recognition of "spirit-

ual laws." We must remember that Calvinism had
known how to combine an awestruck devotion to
the Supreme Being with no very roseate picture
of the destinies of mankind, and for more than
two hundred years had been breeding in the stock
from which Emerson came a willingness to be, as
the phrase is, "damned for the glory of God."

What wonder, then, that when, for the former inexorable dispensation of Providence, Emerson substituted his general spiritual and natural laws, he
should not have felt the spirit of worship fail within
him? On the contrary, his thought moved in the
presence of moral harmonies which seemed to him
truer, more beautiful, and more beneficent than
those of the old theology. An independent philosopher would not have seen in those harmonies an
object of worship or a sufficient basis for optimism.
But he was not an independent philosopher, in spite
of his belief in independence. He inherited the
problems and the preoccupations of the theology
from which he started, being in this respect like
the German idealists, who, with all their pretence of
absolute metaphysics, were in reality only giving
elusive and abstract forms to traditional theology.
Emerson, too, was not primarily a philosopher,
but a Puritan mystic with a poetic fancy and a
gift for observation and epigram, and he saw in the
laws of Nature, idealized by his imagination, only
a more intelligible form of the divinity he had

always recognized and adored. His was not a philosophy passing into a religion, but a religion expressing itself as a philosophy and veiled, as at its setting it descended the heavens, in various tints of poetry and science.

If we ask ourselves what was Emerson's relation to the scientific and religious movements of his time, and what place he may claim in the history of opinion, we must answer that he belonged very little to the past, very little to the present, and almost wholly to that abstract sphere into which mystical or philosophic aspiration has carried a few men in all ages. The religious tradition in which he was reared was that of Puritanism, but of a Puritanism which, retaining its moral intensity and metaphysical abstraction, had minimized its doctrinal expression and become Unitarian. Emerson was indeed the Psyche of Puritanism, "the latest-born and fairest vision far" of all that "faded hierarchy." A Puritan whose religion was all poetry, a poet whose only pleasure was thought, he showed in his life and personality the meagreness, the constraint, the frigid and conscious consecration which belonged to his clerical ancestors, while his inmost impersonal spirit ranged abroad over the fields of history and Nature, gathering what ideas it might, and singing its little snatches of inspired song.

The traditional element was thus rather an external and unessential contribution to Emerson's mind; he had the professional tinge, the decorum, the distinction of an old-fashioned divine; he had also the habit of writing sermons, and he had the national pride and hope of a religious people that felt itself providentially chosen to establish a free and godly commonwealth in a new world. For the rest, he separated himself from the ancient creed of the community with a sense rather of relief than of regret. A literal belief in Christian doctrines repelled him as unspiritual, as manifesting no understanding of the meaning which, as allegories, those doctrines might have to a philosophic and poetical spirit. Although as a clergyman he was at first in the habit of referring to the Bible and its lessons as to a supreme authority, he had no instinctive sympathy with the inspiration of either the Old or the New Testament; in Hafiz or Plutarch, in Plato or Shakespeare, he found more congenial stuff.

While he thus preferred to withdraw, without rancour and without contempt, from the ancient fellowship of the church, he assumed an attitude hardly less cool and deprecatory toward the enthusiasms of the new era. The national ideal of democracy and freedom had his entire sympathy; he allowed himself to be drawn into the movement against slavery; he took a curious and smiling interest in the discoveries of natural science and in the material progress of the age. But he could go no farther. His contemplative nature, his religious training, his dispersed reading, made him stand aside from the life of the world, even while he studied it with benevolent attention. His heart was fixed on eternal things, and he was in no sense a prophet for his age or country. He belonged by nature to that mystical company of devout souls that recognize no particular home and are dispersed throughout history, although not without intercommunication. He felt his affinity to the Hindoos and the Persians, to the Platonists and the Stoics. Like them he remains " a friend and aider of those who would live in the spirit." If not a star of the first magnitude, he is certainly a fixed star in the firmament of philosophy. Alone as yet among Americans, he may be said to have won a place there, if not by the originality of his thought, at least by the originality and beauty of the expression he gave to thoughts that are old and imperishable.

IX

A RELIGION OF DISILLUSION

Man has henceforth this cause of pride: that he has be-thought himself of justice in a universe without justice, and has put justice there. — JEAN LAHOR.

THE break-up of traditional systems and the disappearance of a recognized authority from the religious world have naturally led to many attempts at philosophic reconstruction. Most of these are timid compromises, which leave first principles untouched and contain in a veiled form all the old contradictions. Others are advertisements of some personal notion, some fresh discovery, proposed as a panacea and as an equivalent for all the heritage of human wisdom. A few thinkers, however, inspired by more comprehensive sympathies, and at the same time free from preconceptions, have come nearer to the fundamental elements of the problem and have given out suggestions which, even if not satisfactory in their actual form, are helpful and interesting in their tendency. Such a thinker is the contemporary French poet, Jean Lahor, who, in a volume of thoughts entitled "La gloire du néant," has gathered together three philosophical points of view, we might almost say three religions, and combined their issues in a way which may now seem again new, but which in reality is as old as wisdom.

The form is literary and the outcome in a sense negative; there is no attempt to put new wine into old bottles, no apologetic tone, no unction. Experience is consulted afresh, without preoccupation as to the results of reflection; and if these results are religious, it is because any reasoned appreciation of life is bound to be a religion, even if no conventionally religious elements are imported into the problem. In fact, those prophets who have said that the Sabbath was made for man and who have given moral functions to historical religion, as well as those philosophers who have best understood its nature, have seemed irreligious to their contemporaries, because they have looked upon religion as an interpretation of reality, not as a quasi-reality existing by itself and vouched for merely by tradition and miracle. Religion is an imaginative echo of things natural and moral: and if this echo is to be well attuned, our ear must first be attentive to the natural sounds of which, in religion, we are to develop the harmony.

It is, therefore, not an objection to Jean Lahor's competence to gather for us the elements of a religion that he is a poet rather than a theologian and an observer rather than a philosopher, or that he presents his intuitions without technical apparatus in a series of highly coloured epigrams and little pictures. On the contrary, such simplicity and directness are an advantage when, as in this case, the guiding inspiration is religious. It is religious because, on the one hand, it is imaginative; we are asking ourselves everywhere what Nature says to us and what we are to say in reply; and on the other hand, because it is rational, and these messages and reactions are to be unified into a single science and a single morality. The logical scheme of the system is not made explicit: there is no argumentation and no answers are offered to the objections that might naturally suggest themselves. But the sayings are so arranged and made so to progress in tone and subject that a system of philosophy is clearly implied in them; and the essence of this system is at times briefly expressed.

All, as it behooves a poet, is the transcript of personal experience. We must not look for the inclusion of elements, however important in themselves, which the author has not found in his own life. The omissions are in this case as characteristic as the inclusions. We look in vain, for instance, for any appreciation of Christianity or of all that side of human nature and experience on which faith in Christianity rests; we hear nothing of love and its ideal suggestions, nothing of the aspiration to immortality, nothing of the whole transcendental attitude toward experience. These are grave omissions. They may seem to condemn Jean Lahor, if not as a general philosopher, at least as a representative of an age in which religious thought has so largely centred about these very questions. But our century has been an age of confusion; and a man who at its end wishes to attain some coherence of life and mind, must begin by letting drop much that the age has held in solution. It is by not being an average that a man may become a guide. Only by manifesting the direction of change and embodying that change in his own person can he be a sign of progress. It remains for time to show whether what survives in a given man has fortune on its side and contains the inward elements of vitality. The presumption in this case, when we abstract from our personal prejudices, will seem to be wholly in favour of our author.

The three influences to which he has yielded and which have moulded his mind are the pantheism of the Hindoos, our contemporary natural science, and the ideal of Greek civilization. These three elements might at first sight seem incongruous, and the principle of selection by which they are preferred above all others might seem as hard to find as the principle of union by which they are to be welded into one philosophy. But a little study of these maxims and of the autobiographical sketch which precedes them will, I think, enable us to discover both the principles we miss. The selection of the three influences in question is due to the poetical temperament and scientific tastes of the author, to an individual disposition and to studies which drew him successively to these different sources of instruction. The principle of synthesis, or rather, we should perhaps say, of subordination, by which these various habits of thought are combined in one philosophy, is a moral principle. It is a native power to conceive the ideal and a native loyalty to the ideal when once conceived. This moral enthusiasm is in no sense vapid or sentimental; it hardly comes to the surface in any direct or enthusiastic expression; but it is betrayed and proved to be sincere, now by a passionate pessimism about the natural world, now in detailed and practical demands for a better state of society. A genial individuality and a well-reasoned form of pessimism are, then, the two factors in the development of this interesting thinker, the two keys to the apparently contradictory affinities of his mind.

Our author, as we have said, is a poet, and even if his verses seem at times a little thin and rhetorical, they prove abundantly what is evident also in his prose, namely, that he has keen sensations, that images impress themselves upon him with force, and that any scene whose elements are gorgeous and picturesque or which is weighted with tragic emotion, holds his attention and awakens in him the impulse to literary expression. But this plastic impulse is not powerful, or finds in the environment insufficient support. Great art and great creative achievements are rare in the world, and come for the most part only in those moments and in those places where an unusual concentration of mental energy and the friction of many kindred minds allow the scattered sparks of inspiration to merge and to leap into flame. We need not wonder, therefore, that the æsthetic sensibility of our author is greater than his artistic success. Of which of our contemporaries might we not say the same thing? Jean Lahor's attention is analytic; he is absorbed by his model, he does not absorb it and master it by his art. He has not enough vigour and determination of thought to create eternal forms out of the swift hints of perception. He watches rather passively the flight of his ideas, conscious of their vivacity, of their beauty, but most of all, alas! of their flight. His last word as an observer, his message as a poet, is that all things are illusion. They fade, they pass into one another, the place thereof knows them no more. Nothing of them remains, absolutely nothing, save

the universal indeterminate force that breeds and
devours them perpetually.

A mind thus gifted and thus limited would naturally feel its affinity to Oriental pantheism as soon
as that phase of thought and feeling came within
the radius of its vision. Jean Lahor seems early
to have felt an attraction toward the speculation
of the East, and his prolonged study of that literature could of course only intensify the natural bent
of his mind, and give his thought a more pronounced pantheistic colouring. Had he been wholly
absorbed, however, in such mystical contemplation,
we should have had little to study in him that was
new; only one more case of sensibility and fancy
overpowering a timid intellect, one more gifted
nature arrested at the stage of bewilderment.

But as Jean Lahor is only a pseudonym for the
man, so the sympathy with India which that name
indicates is only one phase of the thinker. Our
poet pursued the study of medicine; he realized in
the concrete the orderly complexities of natural law
and the sordid realities of human life. The vague,
sensuous enthusiasm with which he had followed
the flux of images in his fancy was now sobered by
an accurate knowledge of the miseries, the defeats,
the shames that lie beneath. His poetic sense of
illusion was deepened into a moral sense of wrong.
The same keenness of perception, the same power of
graphic expression, which had made him dwell on

the luxuriance of Nature now made him paint the irony and brutality of life.   There is here and there a touch of bitterness and exaggeration in the satire, as if the man of science felt a personal resentment against a world that had so cheated the poet.

Yet the two descriptions are far from inconsistent; we have merely learned to understand as a process and to conceive as an inner experience what before we had admired as a spectacle.   A scientific view has come to give definition and coherence to phenomena which a poetical pantheism merely saluted as they passed and disappeared into the primordial darkness, or, if you like, into the primordial light.   The two systems differ in tone and in method, but not in result.   Natural science, like pantheism, presents us with a universal flux, in which something, we known not what, moves, we know not why, we know not whither.   The method of this transformation may be more or less accurately described, the general sense of continuity and necessity may find a more or less specific expression in the various fields of experience; yet the outcome is still the same whirligig.   We find ourselves in either case confronted by the same *gloire du néant*, by a nothing that lives and that is beautiful in its nothingness.

These two elements in Jean Lahor's philosophy, the Oriental and the scientific, would thus tend alike to represent man with his intelligence as the pro-

R

duct and the captive of an irrational engine called the universe. Many a man accepts this solution and reconciles himself as best he can to the truth as it appears to him. What is there, he may say, so dreadful in mutability ? What so intolerable in ultimate ignorance ? We know what we need to know, and things last, perhaps, as long as they deserve to last. So, once convinced that his naturalistic philosophy is final, a man will silence the demands of his own reason and call them chimerical. There is nothing to which men, while they have food and drink, cannot reconcile themselves. They will put up with present suffering, with the certainty of death, with solitude, with shame, with wrong, with the expectation of eternal damnation. In the face of such things, they can not only be happy for the moment, but solemnly thank God for having brought them into existence. Habit is stronger than reason, and the respect for fact stronger than the respect for the ideal; nor would the ideal and reason ever prevail did they not make up in persistence what they lack in momentary energy.

It would have been easy, therefore, for Jean Lahor, as for the rest of us, to remain in the naturalistic world, had he had only poetical intuition, or only scientific training, or only both. But there was also in him a third and a moral element, an impulse toward ideal creation, a spark of Promethean fire. He felt a genuine admiration for that humane courage which made the Greeks, for all their clear consciousness of fate, hopeful without illusions and independent without rebellion. In the bosom of the intractable infinite he still distinguished the work of human reason — the cosmos of society, character, and art — like a Noah's ark floating in the Deluge. His imagination had succumbed to the dream of sense; his art had not attempted the task of imposing a meaning or an immortal form upon Nature: but his conscience and his political instinct had held out against the fascinations of Maya. The Greek asserted himself here against the barbarian, the moralist against the naturalist. Nor was this a merely accidental addition or an inconsistency. It was the explicit expression of that creative reason which had all along chafed under the dominion of brute fact and of perpetual illusion. The same moral energy which had made him a pessimist in the presence of Nature made him an idealist at the threshold of life.

For why should the natural world ever come to be called a world of illusion? To call the vivid objects of sense illusory is to compare them to their disadvantage with something else which we conceive as more worthy of the title of reality. This deeper reality must be something ideal, something permanent, something conceived by the intellect, and which only a man having faith in the

intellect could prefer to the objects of sense or
fancy. The Hindoos that our author thinks so
much akin to himself would hardly understand
this rational bias of his thought, this foregone
dissatisfaction with a world of infinite change and
indefinite structure. They would accept as a natural fact that perpetual flux which he emphasizes
as a paradox and laments as a calamity. In spite
of his studied immersion in sensuous illusion, he
is still a native of the sphere of intelligible things,
and it is only the difficulty of finding the permanent beings which he is inclined to look for and
in the presence of which he could alone rest, that
makes him linger with tragic self-consciousness
in the region of fleeting shadows. Accordingly we
need not be surprised by the somewhat forced and
pessimistic note of a pantheism which is really
exotic, and we may be prepared to find the plastic
mind asserting itself ultimately against that system. So Jean Lahor, after the groups of thoughts
which he puts under the title of "L'orient" and
"Le ciel du Nord," adds another group under the
title of "Cosmos."

It would require a philosophical treatise of
greater pretentions than the little book before
us to explain fully how this cosmos can arise out
of the chaos of mechanical forces, and how the
life and the work of reason can be superposed
upon the life of sense and imagination. Our

author's vision, fixed as it is on concrete images
and expressed in detached epigrams, does not
always extend to the philosophical relations of
his thoughts.   Yet he offers, perhaps unconsciously, an admirable variation of that revolution of thought which is associated with the name
of Kant.   He proposes to us as the work of human
intelligence what is commonly believed to be the
work of God.   The universe, apart from us, is a
chaos, but it may be made a cosmos by our efforts
and in our own minds.   The laws of events, apart
from us, are inhuman and irrational, but in the
sphere of human activity they may be dominated
by reason.   We are a part of the blind energy
behind Nature, but by virtue of that energy we impose our purposes on the part of Nature which we
constitute or control.   We can turn from the
stupefying contemplation of an alien universe to
the building of our own house, knowing that, alien
as it is, that universe has chanced to blow its
energy also into our will and to allow itself to
be partially dominated by our intelligence.   Our
mere existence and the modicum of success we
have attained in society, science, and art are the
living proofs of this human power.   The exercise
of this power is the task appointed for us by the
indomitable promptings of our own spirit, a task
in which we need not labour without hope.

For as the various plants and animals have

found foothold and room to grow, maintaining for
long periods the life congenial to them, so the
human race may be able to achieve something like
its perfection and its ideal, maintaining for an
indefinite time all that it values, not by virtue of
an alleged intentional protection of Providence,
but by its own watchful art and exceptional good
fortune. The ideal is itself a function of the
reality and cannot therefore be altogether out of
harmony with the conditions of its own birth
and persistence. Civilization is precarious, but
it need not be short-lived. Its inception is already
a proof that there exists an equilibrium of forces
which is favourable to its existence; and there
is no reason to suppose this equilibrium to be less
stable than that which keeps the planets revolving
in their orbits. There is no impossibility, therefore, in the hope that the human will may have
time to understand itself, and, having understood
itself, to realize the objects of its rational desire.

We see that the "Cosmos" here invoked is
not inconsistent with the "Nothingness" before
described. It is a triumph amid illusions, an order
within chaos, *la gloire du néant*. This hint of a
reconciliation between the practical optimism natural to an active being, and the speculative pessimism inevitable to an intelligent one, is happier
than the muddled solutions of the same problem
with which current philosophies have made us fa

miliar. The philosophy suggested by Jean Lahor is that of Spinoza, if we subtract from the latter its mystical optimism, and add a broad appreciation of human culture. Man cannot attain his happiness by conforming to that which is hostile to himself; he can thus attain only his dissolution. But by using what is hostile to himself for his own ends, as far as his energy extends, he can make an oasis for himself in Nature, and being at peace with himself, be at peace also with her.

Such a view has some relation to the real conditions of human life and progress. What is called the higher optimism, on the contrary, commonly consists in recounting all the evils of existence with a radiant countenance, and telling us that they are all divine ministers of some glorious consummation; but what this consummation is never appears, and we are reduced in practice to a mere glorification of impulse. We are simply invited to accept the conditions of life as they are, and to find in incidental successes a compensation for incidental or — as we should say if we were sincere — for essential failures. Such an optimism impairs by a kind of philosophic Nature-worship that moral loyalty which consists in giving the highest honour to the highest, not to the strongest, things. It substitutes, as pantheism must, the study of tendencies for the study of ends, and the dignity of success for the dignity of justice.

This moral confusion our author avoids by his greater sincerity. He has understood how fundamentally that man is a dupe who does not begin by settling his accounts with Despair. There is no safety in lies; there is no safety even in "postulates." Let the worst of the truth appear, and when it has once seen the light, let it not be immediately wrapped up again in the swaddling clothes of an equivocal rhetoric. In such a disingenuous course there is both temerity and cowardice: temerity in throwing away the opportunity, always afforded by the recognition of fact, of cultivating the real faculties of human nature; cowardice in not being willing to face with patience and dignity the situation in which fate appears to have put us. That Nature is immense, that her laws are mechanical, that the existence and well-being of man upon earth are, from the point of view of the universe, an indifferent incident, — all this is in the first place to be clearly recognized. It is the lesson which both poetic contemplation and practical science had taught Jean Lahor.

Had he stopped to subject his opinion to metaphysical criticism, he would not, I think, have found reason to change it. To subjectify the universe is not to improve it, much less to dissolve it. The space I call my idea has all the properties of the space I called my environment; it has the same inevitable presence and the same fundamental validity.

Because it is a law of our intelligence that two and
two make four, and the implications of that law
may be traced by abstract thought, the world
which is subject to that arithmetical principle is
not made more amenable to our higher demands
than if it had been arithmetical of its own sweet
will. It is not made docile by being called our
creature. Indeed, what is less docile to us than
ourselves? what less subject to our correction than
the foundations of our own being? So when the
Kantian philosophy teaches us to look upon the
enveloping universe as a figment of the understanding and on its laws as results of mental
synthesis and inference, we are still pursued by
the inevitable presence of that figment and confronted involuntarily by that result. Nay, the
conditions of our thought, like the predispositions
of our characters, are the most fatal and inexorable
of our limitations.

Why the world is as it is, whether of itself
or by refraction in the medium of our intellect,
is not a question that affects the practical moralist. What concerns him is that the laws of
the world, whatever their origin, are fixed and
unchangeable conditions of our happiness. We
cannot change the world, even if we boast to have
made it; we must in any case learn to live with it,
whether it be our parent or our child. To veil its
character with euphemisms or to supply its defects

with superstitious assumptions is a course unworthy
of a brave man and abhorrent to a prudent one.
What we should do is to make a modest inven-
tory of our possessions and a just estimate of our
powers in order to apply both, with what strength
we have, to the realization of our ideals in society,
in art, and in science. These will constitute our
Cosmos. In building it — for there is none other
that builds it for us — we shall be carrying on the
work of the only race that has yet seriously attempted to live rationally, the race to which we
owe the name and the idea of a Cosmos, as well as
the beginnings of its realization. We shall then
be making that rare advance in wisdom which consists in abandoning our illusions the better to attain
our ideals.

X

THE ELEMENTS AND FUNCTION OF POETRY

IF a critic, in despair of giving a serious definition of poetry, should be satisfied with saying that poetry is metrical discourse, he would no doubt be giving an inadequate account of the matter, yet not one of which he need be ashamed or which he should regard as superficial. Although a poem be not made by counting of syllables upon the fingers, yet "numbers" is the most poetical synonym we have for verse, and "measure" the most significant equivalent for beauty, for goodness, and perhaps even for truth. Those early and profound philosophers, the followers of Pythagoras, saw the essence of all things in number, and it was by weight, measure, and number, as we read in the Bible, that the Creator first brought Nature out of the void. Every human architect must do likewise with his edifice; he must mould his bricks or hew his stones into symmetrical solids and lay them over one another in regular strata, like a poet's lines.

Measure is a condition of perfection, for perfection requires that order should be pervasive,
that not only the whole before us should have
a form, but that every part in turn should have a
form of its own, and that those parts should be
coördinated among themselves as the whole is
coördinated with the other parts of some greater
cosmos.   Leibnitz lighted in his speculations upon
a conception of organic nature which may be false
as a fact, but which is excellent as an ideal; he
tells us that the difference between living and dead
matter, between animals and machines, is that the
former are composed of parts that are themselves
organic, every portion of the body being itself a
machine, and every portion of that machine still
a machine, and so *ad infinitum;* whereas, in artificial bodies the organization is not in this manner
infinitely deep.   Fine Art, in this as in all things,
imitates the method of Nature and makes its most
beautiful works out of materials that are themselves beautiful.   So that even if the difference between verse and prose consisted only in measure,
that difference would already be analogous to that
between jewels and clay.

The stuff of language is words, and the sensuous
material of words is sound; if language therefore
is to be made perfect, its materials must be made
beautiful by being themselves subjected to a measure, and endowed with a form.   It is true that

language is a symbol for intelligence rather than a stimulus to sense, and accordingly the beauties of discourse which commonly attract attention are merely the beauties of the objects and ideas signified; yet the symbols have a sensible reality of their own, a euphony which appeals to our senses if we keep them open. The tongue will choose those forms of utterance which have a natural grace as mere sound and sensation; the memory will retain these catches, and they will pass and repass through the mind until they become types of instinctive speech and standards of pleasing expression.

The highest form of such euphony is song; the singing voice gives to the sounds it utters the thrill of tonality, — a thrill itself dependent, as we know, on the numerical proportions of the vibrations that it includes. But this kind of euphony and sensuous beauty, the deepest that sounds can have, we have almost wholly surrendered in our speech. Our intelligence has become complex, and language, to express our thoughts, must commonly be more rapid, copious, and abstract than is compatible with singing. Music at the same time has become complex also, and when united with words, at one time disfigures them in the elaboration of its melody, and at another overpowers them in the volume of its sound. So that the art of singing is now in the same plight as that of sculpture, — an abstract and conventional thing surviving by force of tradition and of an innate but now impotent impulse, which under simpler conditions would work itself out into the proper forms of those arts. The truest kind of euphony is thus denied to our poetry. If any verses are still set to music, they are commonly the worst only, chosen for the purpose by musicians of specialized sensibility and inferior intelligence, who seem to be attracted only by tawdry effects of rhetoric and sentiment.

When song is given up, there still remains in speech a certain sensuous quality, due to the nature and order of the vowels and consonants that compose the sounds. This kind of euphony is not neglected by the more dulcet poets, and is now so studied in some quarters that I have heard it maintained by a critic of relative authority that the beauty of poetry consists entirely in the frequent utterance of the sound of "j" and "sh," and the consequent copious flow of saliva in the mouth. But even if saliva is not the whole essence of poetry, there is an unmistakable and fundamental diversity of effect in the various vocalization of different poets, which becomes all the more evident when we compare those who use different languages. One man's speech, or one nation's, is compact, crowded with consonants, rugged, broken with emphatic beats; another man's, or nation's, is open, tripping, rapid, and even. So Byron, mingling in

his boyish fashion burlesque with exquisite sentiment, contrasts English with Italian speech : —

> " I love the language, that soft bastard Latin
> Which melts like kisses from a female mouth
> And sounds as if it should be writ on satin
> With syllables which breathe of the sweet South,
> And gentle liquids gliding all so pat in
> That not a single accent seems uncouth,
> Like our harsh Northern whistling, grunting guttural
> Which we're obliged to hiss and spit and sputter all."

And yet these contrasts, strong when we compare extreme cases, fade from our consciousness in
the actual use of a mother-tongue. The function
makes us unconscious of the instrument, all the
more as it is an indispensable and almost invaria-
ble one. The sense of euphony accordingly attaches
itself rather to another and more variable quality;
the tune, or measure, or rhythm of speech. The
elementary sounds are prescribed by the language
we use, and the selection we may make among those
sounds is limited; but the arrangement of words is
still undetermined, and by casting our speech into
the moulds of metre and rhyme we can give it a
heightened power, apart from its significance. A
tolerable definition of poetry, on its formal side,
might be found in this : that poetry is speech in
which the instrument counts as well as the meaning — poetry is speech for its own sake and for its
own sweetness. As common windows are intended

only to admit the light, but painted windows also to dye it, and to be an object of attention in themselves as well as a cause of visibility in other things, so, while the purest prose is a mere vehicle of thought, verse, like stained glass, arrests attention in its own intricacies, confuses it in its own glories, and is even at times allowed to darken and puzzle in the hope of casting over us a supernatural spell.

Long passages in Shelley's "Revolt of Islam" and Keats' "Endymion" are poetical in this sense; the reader gathers, probably, no definite meaning, but is conscious of a poetic medium, of speech euphonious and measured, and redolent of a kind of objectless passion which is little more than the sensation of the movement and sensuous richness of the lines. Such poetry is not great; it has, in fact, a tedious vacuity, and is unworthy of a mature mind; but it is poetical, and could be produced only by a legitimate child of the Muse. It belongs to an apprenticeship, but in this case the apprenticeship of genius. It bears that relation to great poems which scales and aimless warblings bear to great singing — they test the essential endowment and fineness of the organ which is to be employed in the art. Without this sensuous background and ingrained predisposition to beauty, no art can reach the deepest and most exquisite effects; and even without an intelligible superstructure these sensuous qualities suffice to give that thrill of exaltation, that suggestion of an ideal world, which we feel in the presence of any true beauty.

The sensuous beauty of words and their utterance in measure suffice, therefore, for poetry of one sort — where these are there is something unmistakably poetical, although the whole of poetry, or the best of poetry, be not yet there. Indeed, in such works as " The Revolt of Islam " or " Endymion " there is already more than mere metre and sound; there is the colour and choice of words, the fanciful, rich, or exquisite juxtaposition of phrases. The vocabulary and the texture of the style are precious; affected, perhaps, but at any rate refined.

This quality, which is that almost exclusively exploited by the Symbolist, we may call euphuism — the choice of coloured words and rare and elliptical phrases. If great poets are like architects and sculptors, the euphuists are like goldsmiths and jewellers; their work is filigree in precious metals, encrusted with glowing stones. Now euphuism contributes not a little to the poetic effect of the tirades of Keats and Shelley; if we wish to see the power of versification without euphuism we may turn to the tirades of Pope, where metre and euphony are displayed alone, and we have the outline or skeleton of poetry without the filling.

> " In spite of pride, in erring reason's spite,
> One truth is clear, Whatever is, is right."

s

We should hesitate to say that such writing was truly poetical; so that some euphuism would seem to be necessary as well as metre, to the formal essence of poetry.

An example of this sort, however, takes us out of the merely verbal into the imaginative region; the reason that Pope is hardly poetical to us is not that he is inharmonious, — not a defect of euphony, — but that he is too intellectual and has an excess of mentality. It is easier for words to be poetical without any thought, when they are felt merely as sensuous and musical, than for them to remain so when they convey an abstract notion, — especially if that notion be a tart and frigid sophism, like that of the couplet just quoted. The pyrotechnics of the intellect then take the place of the glow of sense, and the artifice of thought chills the pleasure we might have taken in the grace of expression.

If poetry in its higher reaches is more philosophical than history, because it presents the memorable types of men and things apart from unmeaning circumstances, so in its primary substance and texture poetry is more philosophical than prose because it is nearer to our immediate experience. Poetry breaks up the trite conceptions designated by current words into the sensuous qualities out of which those conceptions were originally put together. We name what we conceive and believe in, not what we see; things, not images; souls, not voices and silhouettes. This naming, with the whole education of the senses which it accompanies, subserves the uses of life; in order to thread our way through the labyrinth of objects which assault us, we must make a great selection in our sensuous experience; half of what we see and hear we must pass over as insignificant, while we piece out the other half with such an ideal complement as is necessary to turn it into a fixed and well-ordered world. This labour of perception and understanding, this spelling of the material meaning of experience is enshrined in our work-a-day language and ideas; ideas which are literally poetic in the sense that they are "made" (for every conception in an adult mind is a fiction), but which are at the same time prosaic because they are made economically, by abstraction, and for use.

When the child of poetic genius, who has learned this intellectual and utilitarian language in the cradle, goes afield and gathers for himself the aspects of Nature, he begins to encumber his mind with the many living impressions which the intellect rejected, and which the language of the intellect can hardly convey; he labours with his nameless burden of perception, and wastes himself in aimless impulses of emotion and revery, until finally the method of some art offers a vent to his inspiration, or to such part of it as can survive the test of time and the discipline of expression.

The poet retains by nature the innocence of the eye, or recovers it easily; he disintegrates the fictions of common perception into their sensuous elements, gathers these together again into chance groups as the accidents of his environment or the affinities of his temperament may conjoin them; and this wealth of sensation and this freedom of fancy, which make an extraordinary ferment in his ignorant heart, presently bubble over into some kind of utterance.

The fulness and sensuousness of such effusions bring them nearer to our actual perceptions than common discourse could come; yet they may easily seem remote, overloaded, and obscure to those accustomed to think entirely in symbols, and never to be interrupted in the algebraic rapidity of their thinking by a moment's pause and examination of heart, nor ever to plunge for a moment into that torrent of sensation and imagery over which the bridge of prosaic associations habitually carries us safe and dry to some conventional act. How slight that bridge commonly is, how much an affair of trestles and wire, we can hardly conceive until we have trained ourselves to an extreme sharpness of introspection. But psychologists have discovered, what laymen generally will confess, that we hurry by the procession of our mental images as we do by the traffic of the street, intent on business, gladly forgetting the noise and movement of the scene.

and looking only for the corner we would turn or
the door we would enter.   Yet in our alertest
moment the depths of the soul are still dreaming;
the real world stands drawn in bare outline against
a background of chaos and unrest.   Our logical
thoughts dominate experience only as the paral-
lels and meridians make a checker-board of the
sea.   They guide our voyage without controlling
the waves, which toss for ever in spite of our ability
to ride over them to our chosen ends.   Sanity is a
madness put to good uses; waking life is a dream
controlled.

Out of the neglected riches of this dream the
poet fetches his wares.   He dips into the chaos
that underlies the rational shell of the world and
brings up some superfluous image, some emotion
dropped by the way, and reattaches it to the
present object; he reinstates things unnecessary,
he emphasizes things ignored, he paints in again
into the landscape the tints which the intellect has
allowed to fade from it.   If he seems sometimes
to obscure a fact, it is only because he is restoring
an experience.   We may observe this process in
the simplest cases.   When Ossian, mentioning the
sun, says it is round as the shield of his fathers,
the expression is poetical.   Why?   Because he
has added to the word sun, in itself sufficient and
unequivocal, other words, unnecessary for practical
clearness, but serving to restore the individuality

of his perception and its associations in his mind. There is no square sun with which the sun he is speaking of could be confused; to stop and call it round is a luxury, a halting in the sensation for the love of its form. And to go on to tell us, what is wholly impertinent, that the shield of his fathers was round also, is to invite us to follow the chance wanderings of his fancy, to give us a little glimpse of the stuffing of his own brain, or, we might almost say, to turn over the pattern of his embroidery and show us the loose threads hanging out on the wrong side. Such an escapade disturbs and interrupts the true vision of the object, and a great poet, rising to a perfect conception of the sun and forgetting himself, would have disdained to make it; but it has a romantic and pathological interest, it restores an experience, and is in that measure poetical. We have been made to halt at the sensation, and to penetrate for a moment into its background of dream.

But it is not only thoughts or images that the poet draws in this way from the store of his experience, to clothe the bare form of conventional objects: he often adds to these objects a more subtle ornament, drawn from the same source. For the first element which the intellect rejects in forming its ideas of things is the emotion which accompanies the perception; and this emotion is the first thing the poet restores. He stops at the image, because he stops to enjoy. He wanders into the by-paths of association because the by-paths are delightful. The love of beauty which made him give measure and cadence to his words, the love of harmony which made him rhyme them, reappear in his imagination and make him select there also the material that is itself beautiful, or capable of assuming beautiful forms. The link that binds together the ideas, sometimes so wide apart, which his wit assimilates, is most often the link of emotion; they have in common some element of beauty or of horror.

The poet's art is to a great extent the art of intensifying emotions by assembling the scattered objects that naturally arouse them. He sees the affinities of things by seeing their common affinities with passion. As the guiding principle of practical thinking is some interest, so that only what is pertinent to that interest is selected by the attention; as the guiding principle of scientific thinking is some connection of things in time or space, or some identity of law; so in poetic thinking the guiding principle is often a mood or a quality of sentiment. By this union of disparate things having a common overtone of feeling, the feeling is itself evoked in all its strength; nay, it is often created for the first time, much as by a new mixture of old pigments Perugino could produce the unprecedented limpidity of his colour, or Titian the un-

precedented glow of his. Poets can thus arouse
sentiments finer than any which they have known,
and in the act of composition become discoverers
of new realms of delightfulness and grief. Expression is a misleading term which suggests that
something previously known is rendered or imi-
tated; whereas the expression is itself an original
fact, the values of which are then referred to the
thing expressed, much as the honours of a Chinese
mandarin are attributed retroactively to his parents. So the charm which a poet, by his art of
combining images and shades of emotion, casts over
a scene or an action, is attached to the principal
actor in it, who gets the benefit of the setting
furnished him by a well-stocked mind.

The poet is himself subject to this illusion, and
a great part of what is called poetry, although by
no means the best part of it, consists in this sort
of idealization by proxy. We dye the world of
our own colour; by a pathetic fallacy, by a false
projection of sentiment, we soak Nature with our
own feeling, and then celebrate her tender sympathy with our moral being. This aberration, as
we see in the case of Wordsworth, is not inconsistent with a high development of both the faculties which it confuses, — I mean vision and feeling.
On the contrary, vision and feeling, when most
abundant and original, most easily present themselves in this undivided form. There would be

need of a force of intellect which poets rarely possess to rationalize their inspiration without diminishing its volume: and if, as is commonly the case, the energy of the dream and the passion in them is greater than that of the reason, and they cannot attain true propriety and supreme beauty in their works, they can, nevertheless, fill them with lovely images and a fine moral spirit.

The pouring forth of both perceptive and emotional elements in their mixed and indiscriminate form gives to this kind of imagination the directness and truth which sensuous poetry possesses on a lower level. The outer world bathed in the hues of human feeling, the inner world expressed in the forms of things, — that is the primitive condition of both before intelligence and the prosaic classification of objects have abstracted them and assigned them to their respective spheres. Such identifications, on which a certain kind of metaphysics prides itself also, are not discoveries of profound genius; they are exactly like the observation of Ossian that the sun is round and that the shield of his fathers was round too; they are disintegrations of conventional objects, so that the original associates of our perceptions reappear; then the thing and the emotion which chanced to be simultaneous are said to be one, and we return, unless a better principle of organization is substituted for the principle abandoned, to the chaos of a passive animal consciousness, where all is mixed together, projected together, and felt as an unutterable whole.

The pathetic fallacy is a return to that early habit of thought by which our ancestors peopled the world with benevolent and malevolent spirits; what they felt in the presence of objects they took to be a part of the objects themselves. In returning to this natural confusion, poetry does us a service in that she recalls and consecrates those phases of our experience which, as useless to the understanding of material reality, we are in danger of forgetting altogether. Therein is her vitality, for she pierces to the quick and shakes us out of our servile speech and imaginative poverty; she reminds us of all we have felt, she invites us even to dream a little, to nurse the wonderful spontaneous creations which at every waking moment we are snuffing out in our brain. And the indulgence is no mere momentary pleasure; much of its exuberance clings afterward to our ideas; we see the more and feel the more for that exercise; we are capable of finding greater entertainment in the common aspects of Nature and life. When the veil of convention is once removed from our eyes by the poet, we are better able to dominate any particular experience and, as it were, to change its scale, now losing ourselves in its infinitesimal texture, now in its infinite ramifications.

If the function of poetry, however, did not go beyond this recovery of sensuous and imaginative freedom, at the expense of disrupting our useful habits of thought, we might be grateful to it for occasionally relieving our numbness, but we should have to admit that it was nothing but a relaxation; that spiritual discipline was not to be gained from it in any degree, but must be sought wholly in that intellectual system that builds the science of Nature with the categories of prose. So conceived, poetry would deserve the judgment passed by Plato on all the arts of flattery and entertainment; it might be crowned as delightful, but must be either banished altogether as meretricious or at least confined to a few forms and occasions where it might do little harm. The judgment of Plato has been generally condemned by philosophers, although it is eminently rational, and justified by the simplest principles of morals. It has been adopted instead, although unwittingly, by the practical and secular part of mankind, who look upon artists and poets as inefficient and brainsick people under whose spell it would be a serious calamity to fall, although they may be called in on feast days as an ornament and luxury together with the cooks, hairdressers, and florists.

Several circumstances, however, might suggest

to us the possibility that the greatest function of poetry may be still to find.   Plato, while condemning Homer, was a kind of poet himself; his quarrel with the followers of the Muse was not a quarrel with the goddess; and the good people of Philistia, distrustful as they may be of profane art, pay undoubting honour to religion, which is a kind of poetry as much removed from their sphere as the midnight revels upon Mount Citheron, which, to be sure, were also religious in their inspiration. Why, we may ask, these apparent inconsistencies? Why do our practical men make room for religion in the background of their world?   Why did Plato, after banishing the poets, poetize the universe in his prose?   Because the abstraction by which the world of science and of practice is drawn out of our experience, is too violent to satisfy even the thoughtless and vulgar; the ideality of the machine we call Nature, the conventionality of the drama we call the world, are too glaring not to be somehow perceived by all.   Each must sometimes fall back upon the soul; he must challenge this apparition with the thought of death; he must ask himself for the mainspring and value of his life.   He will then remember his stifled loves; he will feel that only his illusions have ever given him a sense of reality, only his passions the hope and the vision of peace.   He will read himself through and almost gather a meaning from his experience; at least he will half believe that all he has been dealing with was a dream and a symbol, and raise his eyes toward the truth beyond.

This plastic moment of the mind, when we become aware of the artificiality and inadequacy of what common sense perceives, is the true moment of poetic opportunity, — an opportunity, we may hasten to confess, which is generally missed. The strain of attention, the concentration and focussing of thought on the unfamiliar immediacy of things, usually brings about nothing but confusion. We are dazed, we are filled with a sense of unutterable things, luminous yet indistinguishable, many yet one. Instead of rising to imagination, we sink into mysticism.

To accomplish a mystical disintegration is not the function of any art; if any art seems to accomplish it, the effect is only incidental, being involved, perhaps, in the process of constructing the proper object of that art, as we might cut down trees and dig them up by the roots to lay the foundations of a temple. For every art looks to the building up of something. And just because the world built up by common sense and natural science is an inadequate world (a skeleton which needs the filling of sensation before it can live), therefore the moment when we realize its inadequacy is the moment when the higher arts find their opportunity. When the world is shattered to bits they can come and "build it nearer to the heart's desire."

The great function of poetry, which we have not yet directly mentioned, is precisely this: to repair to the material of experience, seizing hold of the reality of sensation and fancy beneath the surface of conventional ideas, and then out of that living but indefinite material to build new structures, richer, finer, fitter to the primary tendencies of our nature, truer to the ultimate possibilities of the soul. Our descent into the elements of our being is then justified by our subsequent freer ascent toward its goal: we revert to sense only to find food for reason; we destroy conventions only to construct ideals.

Such analysis for the sake of creation is the essence of all great poetry. Science and common sense are themselves in their way poets of no mean order, since they take the material of experience and make out of it a clear, symmetrical, and beautiful world; the very propriety of this art, however, has made it common. Its figures have become mere rhetoric and its metaphors prose. Yet, even as it is, a scientific and mathematical vision has a higher beauty than the irrational poetry of sensation and impulse, which merely tickles the brain, like liquor, and plays upon our random, imaginative lusts. The imagination of a great poet, on the contrary, is as orderly as that of an astronomer, and as large; he has the naturalist's patience, the naturalist's love of detail and eye trained to see fine gradations and essential lines; he knows no hurry; he has no pose, no sense of originality; he finds his effects in his subject, and his subject in his inevitable world. Resembling the naturalist in all this, he differs from him in the balance of his interests; the poet has the concreter mind; his visible world wears all its colours and retains its indwelling passion and life. Instead of studying in experience its calculable elements, he studies its moral values, its beauty, the openings it offers to the soul: and the cosmos he constructs is accordingly an ideal theatre for the spirit in which its noblest potential drama is enacted and its destiny resolved.

This supreme function of poetry is only the consummation of the method by which words and imagery are transformed into verse. As verse breaks up the prosaic order of syllables and subjects them to a recognizable and pleasing measure, so poetry breaks up the whole prosaic picture of experience to introduce into it a rhythm more congenial and intelligible to the mind. And in both these cases the operation is essentially the same as that by which, in an intermediate sphere, the images rejected by practical thought, and the emotions ignored by it, are so marshalled as to fill the mind with a truer and intenser consciousness of its memorable experience. The poetry of fancy, of observation, and of passion moves on this intermediate level; the poetry of mere sound and virtuosity is confined to the lower sphere; and the highest is reserved for the poetry of the creative reason. But one principle is present throughout,— the principle of Beauty, — the art of assimilating phenomena, whether words, images, emotions, or systems of ideas, to the deeper innate cravings of the mind.

Let us now dwell a little on this higher function of poetry and try to distinguish some of its phases.

The creation of characters is what many of us might at first be tempted to regard as the supreme triumph of the imagination. If we abstract, however, from our personal tastes and look at the matter in its human and logical relations, we shall see, I think, that the construction of characters is not the ultimate task of poetic fiction. A character can never be exhaustive of our materials: for it exists by its idiosyncrasy, by its contrast with other natures, by its development of one side, and one side only, of our native capacities. It is, therefore, not by characterization as such that the ultimate message can be rendered. The poet can put only a part of himself into any of his heroes, but he must put the whole into his noblest work. A character is accordingly only a fragmentary unity;

fragmentary in respect to its origin, — since it is conceived by enlargement, so to speak, of a part of our own being to the exclusion of the rest, — and fragmentary in respect to the object it presents, since a character must live in an environment and be appreciated by contrast and by the sense of derivation. Not the character, but its effects and causes, is the truly interesting thing. Thus in master poets, like Homer and Dante, the characters, although well drawn, are subordinate to the total movement and meaning of the scene. There is indeed something pitiful, something comic, in any comprehended soul; souls, like other things, are only definable by their limitations. We feel instinctively that it would be insulting to speak of any man to his face as we should speak of him in his absence, even if what we say is in the way of praise: for absent he is a character understood, but present he is a force respected.

In the construction of ideal characters, then, the imagination is busy with material, — particular actions and thoughts, — which suggest their unification in persons; but the characters thus conceived can hardly be adequate to the profusion of our observations, nor exhaustive, when all personalities are taken together, of the interest of our lives. Characters are initially imbedded in life, as the gods themselves are originally imbedded in Nature. Poetry must, therefore, to render all

T

reality, render also the background of its figures, and the events that condition their acts. We must place them in that indispensable environment which the landscape furnishes to the eye and the social medium to the emotions.

The visible landscape is not a proper object for poetry. Its elements, and especially the emotional stimulation which it gives, may be suggested or expressed in verse; but landscape is not thereby represented in its proper form; it appears only as an element and associate of moral unities. Painting, architecture, and gardening, with the art of stage setting, have the visible landscape for their object, and to those arts we may leave it. But there is a sort of landscape larger than the visible, which escapes the synthesis of the eye; it is present to that topographical sense by which we always live in the consciousness that there is a sea, that there are mountains, that the sky is above us, even when we do not see it, and that the tribes of men, with their different degrees of blamelessness, are scattered over the broad-backed earth. This cosmic landscape poetry alone can render, and it is no small part of the art to awaken the sense of it at the right moment, so that the object that occupies the centre of vision may be seen in its true lights, coloured by its wider associations, and dignified by its felt affinities to things permanent and great. As the Italian masters were wont not to paint their groups of saints about the Virgin without enlarging the canvas, so as to render a broad piece of sky, some mountains and rivers, and nearer, perhaps, some decorative pile; so the poet of larger mind envelops his characters in the atmosphere of Nature and history, and keeps us constantly aware of the world in which they move.

The distinction of a poet — the dignity and humanity of his thought — can be measured by nothing, perhaps, so well as by the diameter of the world in which he lives; if he is supreme, his vision, like Dante's, always stretches to the stars. And Virgil, a supreme poet sometimes unjustly belittled, shows us the same thing in another form; his landscape is the Roman universe, his theme the sacred springs of Roman greatness in piety, constancy, and law. He has not written a line in forgetfulness that he was a Roman; he loves country life and its labours because he sees in it the origin and bulwark of civic greatness; he honours tradition because it gives perspective and momentum to the history that ensues; he invokes the gods, because they are symbols of the physical and moral forces by which Rome struggled to dominion.

Almost every classic poet has the topographical sense; he swarms with proper names and allusions to history and fable; if an epithet is to be thrown in anywhere to fill up the measure of a line, he chooses instinctively an appellation of place or

family; his wine is not red, but Samian; his gorges
are not deep, but are the gorges of Hæmus; his
songs are not sweet, but Pierian. We may deride
their practice as conventional, but they could far
more justly deride ours as insignificant. Conventions do not arise without some reason, and genius
will know how to rise above them by a fresh appreciation of their rightness, and will feel no
temptation to overturn them in favour of personal whimsies. The ancients found poetry not
so much in sensible accidents as in essential forms
and noble associations; and this fact marks very
clearly their superior education. They dominated
the world as we no longer dominate it, and lived, as
we are too distracted to live, in the presence of the
rational and the important.

A physical and historical background, however,
is of little moment to the poet in comparison with
that other environment of his characters, — the
dramatic situations in which they are involved.
The substance of poetry is, after all, emotion; and
if the intellectual emotion of comprehension and
the mimetic one of impersonation are massive,
they are not so intense as the appetites and other
transitive emotions of life; the passions are the
chief basis of all interests, even the most ideal,
and the passions are seldom brought into play
except by the contact of man with man. The
various forms of love and hate are only possible

in society, and to imagine occasions in which these
feelings may manifest all their inward vitality is
the poet's function,—one in which he follows the
fancy of every child, who puffs himself out in his
day-dreams into an endless variety of heroes and
lovers. The thrilling adventures which he craves
demand an appropriate theatre; the glorious emotions with which he bubbles over must at all haz-
ards find or feign their correlative objects.

But the passions are naturally blind, and the
poverty of the imagination, when left alone, is
absolute. The passions may ferment as they will,
they never can breed an idea out of their own
energy. This idea must be furnished by the
senses, by outward experience, else the hunger
of the soul will gnaw its own emptiness for ever.
Where the seed of sensation has once fallen, however, the growth, variations, and exuberance of
fancy may be unlimited. Only we still observe
(as in the child, in dreams, and in the poetry of
ignorant or mystical poets) that the intensity of
inwardly generated visions does not involve any
real increase in their scope or dignity. The inex-
perienced mind remains a thin mind, no matter
how much its vapours may be heated and blown
about by natural passion. It was a capital error
in Fichte and Schopenhauer to assign essential
fertility to the will in the creation of ideas. They
mistook, as human nature will do, even when at

times it professes pessimism, an ideal for a reality: and because they saw how much the will
clings to its objects, how it selects and magnifies
them, they imagined that it could breed them out
of itself. A man who thinks clearly will see that
such self-determination of a will is inconceivable,
since what has no external relation and no diversity of structure cannot of itself acquire diversity
of functions. Such inconceivability, of course, need
not seem a great objection to a man of impassioned
inspiration; he may even claim a certain consistency in positing, on the strength of his preference,
the inconceivable to be a truth.

The alleged fertility of the will is, however, dis-
proved by experience, from which metaphysics must
in the end draw its analogies and plausibility.
The passions discover, they do not create, their
occasions; a fact which is patent when we observe
how they seize upon what objects they find, and
how reversible, contingent, and transferable the
emotions are in respect to their objects. A doll
will be loved instead of a child, a child instead of
a lover, God instead of everything. The differentiation of the passions, as far as consciousness is
concerned, depends on the variety of the objects
of experience,—that is, on the differentiation of
the senses and of the environment which stimulates them.

When the "infinite" spirit enters the human

body, it is determined to certain limited forms
of life by the organs which it wears; and its
blank potentiality becomes actual in thought and
deed, according to the fortunes and relations of
its organism. The ripeness of the passions may
thus precede the information of the mind and
lead to groping in by-paths without issue; a phenomenon which appears not only in the obscure
individual whose abnormalities the world ignores,
but also in the starved, half-educated genius that
pours the whole fire of his soul into trivial arts
or grotesque superstitions. The hysterical forms
of music and religion are the refuge of an idealism that has lost its way; the waste and failures
of life flow largely in those channels. The carnal
temptations of youth are incidents of the same
maladaptation, when passions assert themselves
before the conventional order of society can allow
them physical satisfaction, and long before philosophy or religion can hope to transform them into
fuel for its own sacrificial flames.

Hence flows the greatest opportunity of fiction.
We have, in a sense, an infinite will; but we have
a limited experience, an experience sadly inadequate
to exercise that will either in its purity or its
strength. To give form to our capacities nothing
is required but the appropriate occasion; this the
poet, studying the world, will construct for us out
of the materials of his observations. He will in-

volve us in scenes which lie beyond the narrow
lane of our daily ploddings; he will place us in
the presence of important events, that we may feel
our spirit rise momentarily to the height of his
great argument.   The possibilities of love or glory,
of intrigue and perplexity, will be opened up before us; if he gives us a good plot, we can readily
furnish the characters, because each of them will be
the realization of some stunted potential self of
our own.   It is by the plot, then, that the characters will be vivified, because it is by the plot that
our own character will be expanded into its latent
possibilities.

The description of an alien character can serve
this purpose only very imperfectly; but the presentation of the circumstances in which that character
manifests itself will make description unnecessary, since our instinct will supply all that is requisite for the impersonation.   Thus it seems that
Aristotle was justified in making the plot the chief
element in fiction: for it is by virtue of the plot
that the characters live, or, rather, that we live in
them, and by virtue of the plot accordingly that
our soul rises to that imaginative activity by which
we tend at once to escape from the personal life
and to realize its ideal.   This idealization is, of
course, partial and merely relative to the particular
adventure in which we imagine ourselves engaged.
But in some single direction our will finds self-

expression, and understands itself; runs through the career which it ignorantly coveted, and gathers the fruits and the lesson of that enterprise.

This is the essence of tragedy: the sense of the finished life, of the will fulfilled and enlightened: that purging of the mind so much debated upon, which relieves us of pent-up energies, transfers our feelings to a greater object, and thus justifies and entertains our dumb passions, detaching them at the same time for a moment from their accidental occasions in our earthly life. An episode, however lurid, is not a tragedy in this nobler sense, because it does not work itself out to the end; it pleases without satisfying, or shocks without enlightening. This enlightenment, I need hardly say, is not a matter of theory or of moral maxims; the enlightenment by which tragedy is made sublime is a glimpse into the ultimate destinies of our will. This discovery need not be an ethical gain—Macbeth and Othello attain it as much as Brutus and Hamlet—it may serve to accentuate despair, or cruelty, or indifference, or merely to fill the imagination for a moment without much affecting the permanent tone of the mind. But without such a glimpse of the goal of a passion the passion has not been adequately read, and the fiction has served to amuse us without really enlarging the frontiers of our ideal experience. Memory and emotion have been played upon, but imagination has not brought anything new to the light.

The dramatic situation, however, gives us the environment of a single passion, of life in one of its particular phases; and although a passion, like Romeo's love, may seem to devour the whole soul, and its fortunes may seem to be identical with those of the man, yet much of the man, and the best part of him, goes by the board in such a simplification. If Leonardo da Vinci, for example, had met in his youth with Romeo's fate, his end would have been no more ideally tragic than if he had died at eighteen of a fever; we should be touched rather by the pathos of what he had missed, than by the sublimity of what he had experienced. A passion like Romeo's, compared with the ideal scope of human thought and emotion, is a thin dream, a pathological crisis.

Accordingly Aristophanes, remembering the original religious and political functions of tragedy, blushes to see upon the boards a woman in love. And we should readily agree with him, but for two reasons,—one, that we abstract too much, in our demands upon art, from nobility of mind, and from the thought of totality and proportion; the other, that we have learned to look for a symbolic meaning in detached episodes, and to accept the incidental emotions they cause, because of their violence and our absorption in them, as in some sense sacramental and representative of the whole. Thus the picture of an unmeaning passion, of a crime with-

out an issue, does not appear to our romantic apprehension as the sorry farce it is, but rather as a true
tragedy.   Some have lost even the capacity to conceive of a true tragedy, because they have no idea
of a cosmic order, of general laws of life, or of an
impersonal religion.   They measure the profundity
of feeling by its intensity, not by its justifying
relations; and in the radical disintegration of their
spirit, the more they are devoured the more they
fancy themselves fed.   But the majority of us
retain some sense of a meaning in our joys and
sorrows, and even if we cannot pierce to their ultimate object, we feel that what absorbs us here and
now has a merely borrowed or deputed power; that
it is a symbol and foretaste of all reality speaking
to the whole soul.   At the same time our intelligence is too confused to give us any picture of
that reality, and our will too feeble to marshal our
disorganized loves into a religion consistent with
itself and harmonious with the comprehended universe.   A rational ideal eludes us, and we are the
more inclined to plunge into mysticism.

Nevertheless, the function of poetry, like that of
science, can only be fulfilled by the conception of
harmonies that become clearer as they grow richer.
As the chance note that comes to be supported by
a melody becomes in that melody determinate and
necessary, and as the melody, when woven into a
harmony, is explicated in that harmony and fixed

beyond recall; so the single emotion, the fortuitous dream, launched by the poet into the world of recognizable and immortal forms, looks in that world for its ideal supports and affinities. It must find them or else be blown back among the ghosts. The highest ideality is the comprehension of the real. Poetry is not at its best when it depicts a further possible experience, but when it initiates us, by feigning something which as an experience is impossible, into the meaning of the experience which we have actually had.

The highest example of this kind of poetry is religion; and although disfigured and misunderstood by the simplicity of men who believe in it without being capable of that imaginative interpretation of life in which its truth consists, yet this religion is even then often beneficent, because it colours life harmoniously with the ideal. Religion may falsely represent the ideal as a reality, but we must remember that the ideal, if not so represented, would be despised by the majority of men, who cannot understand that the value of things is moral, and who therefore attribute to what is moral a natural existence, thinking thus to vindicate its importance and value. But value lies in meaning, not in substance; in the ideal which things approach, not in the energy which they embody.

The highest poetry, then, is not that of the versifiers, but that of the prophets, or of such poets as interpret verbally the visions which the prophets have rendered in action and sentiment rather than in adequate words. That the intuitions of religion are poetical, and that in such intuitions poetry has its ultimate function, are truths of which both religion and poetry become more conscious the more they advance in refinement and profundity. A crude and superficial theology may confuse God with the thunder, the mountains, the heavenly bodies, or the whole universe; but when we pass from these easy identifications to a religion that has taken root in history and in the hearts of men, and has come to flower, we find its objects and its dogmas purely ideal, transparent expressions of moral experience and perfect counterparts of human needs. The evidence of history or of the senses is left far behind and never thought of; the evidence of the heart, the value of the idea, are alone regarded.

Take, for instance, the doctrine of transubstantiation. A metaphor here is the basis of a dogma, because the dogma rises to the same subtle region as the metaphor, and gathers its sap from the same soil of emotion. Religion has here rediscovered its affinity with poetry, and in insisting on the truth of its mystery it unconsciously vindicates the ideality of its truth. Under the accidents of bread and wine lies, says the dogma, the substance of Christ's body, blood, and divinity. What is that but to treat facts as an appearance, and their ideal import as a reality? And to do this is the very essence of poetry, for which everything visible is a sacrament—an outward sign of that inward grace for which the soul is thirsting.

In this same manner, where poetry rises from its elementary and detached expressions in rhythm, euphuism, characterization, and story-telling, and comes to the consciousness of its highest function, that of portraying the ideals of experience and destiny, then the poet becomes aware that he is essentially a prophet, and either devotes himself, like Homer or Dante, to the loving expression of the religion that exists, or like Lucretius or Wordsworth, to the heralding of one which he believes to be possible. Such poets are aware of their highest mission; others, whatever the energy of their genius, have not conceived their ultimate function as poets. They have been willing to leave their world ugly as a whole, after stuffing it with a sufficient profusion of beauties. Their contemporaries, their fellow-countrymen for many generations, may not perceive this defect, because they are naturally even less able than the poet himself to understand the necessity of so large a harmony. If he is short-sighted, they are blind, and his poetic world may seem to them sublime in its significance, because it may suggest some partial lifting of their daily burdens and some partial idealization of their incoherent thoughts.

Such insensibility to the highest poetry is no more extraordinary than the corresponding indifference to the highest religion; nobility and excellence, however, are not dependent on the suffrage of half-baked men, but on the original disposition of the clay and the potter; I mean on the conditions of the art and the ideal capacities of human nature. Just as a note is better than a noise because, its beats being regular, the ear and brain can react with pleasure on that regularity, so all the stages of harmony are better than the confusion out of which they come, because the soul that perceives that harmony welcomes it as the fulfilment of her natural ends. The Pythagoreans were therefore right when they made number the essence of the knowable world, and Plato was right when he said harmony was the first condition of the highest good. The good man is a poet whose syllables are deeds and make a harmony in Nature. The poet is a rebuilder of the imagination, to make a harmony in that. And he is not a complete poet if his whole imagination is not attuned and his whole experience composed into a single symphony.

For his complete equipment, then, it is necessary, in the first place, that he sing; that his voice be pure and well pitched, and that his numbers flow; then, at a higher stage, his images must fit with one another; he must be euphuistic, colouring his thoughts with many reflected lights of memory and suggestion, so that their harmony may be rich and profound; again, at a higher stage, he must be sensuous and free, that is, he must build up his world with the primary elements of experience, not with the conventions of common sense or intelligence; he must draw the whole soul into his harmonies, even if in doing so he disintegrates the partial systematizations of experience made by abstract science in the categories of prose. But finally, this disintegration must not leave the poet weltering in a chaos of sense and passion; it must be merely the ploughing of the ground before a new harvest, the kneading of the clay before the modelling of a more perfect form. The expression of emotion should be rationalized by derivation from character and by reference to the real objects that arouse it—to Nature, to history, and to the universe of truth; the experience imagined should be conceived as a destiny, governed by principles, and issuing in the discipline and enlightenment of the will. In this way alone can poetry become an interpretation of life and not merely an irrelevant excursion into the realm of fancy, multiplying our images without purpose, and distracting us from our business without spiritual gain.

If we may then define poetry, not in the formal sense of giving the minimum of what may be called by that name, but in the ideal sense of determining the goal which it approaches and the achievement

in which all its principles would be fulfilled, we
may say that poetry is metrical and euphuistic discourse, expressing thought which is both sensuous
and ideal.

Such is poetry as a literary form; but if we drop
the limitation to verbal expression, and think of
poetry as that subtle fire and inward light which
seems at times to shine through the world and
to touch the images in our minds with ineffable
beauty, then poetry is a momentary harmony in
the soul amid stagnation or conflict,—a glimpse
of the divine and an incitation to a religious
life.

Religion is poetry become the guide of life,
poetry substituted for science or supervening upon
it as an approach to the highest reality. Poetry
is religion allowed to drift, left without points of
application in conduct and without an expression
in worship and dogma; it is religion without practical efficacy and without metaphysical illusion.
The ground of this abstractness of poetry, however, is usually only its narrow scope; a poet who
plays with an idea for half an hour, or constructs
a character to which he gives no profound moral
significance, forgets his own thought, or remembers
it only as a fiction of his leisure, because he has
not dug his well deep enough to tap the subterraneous springs of his own life. But when the poet
enlarges his theatre and puts into his rhapsodies

the true visions of his people and of his soul, his poetry is the consecration of his deepest convictions, and contains the whole truth of his religion. What the religion of the vulgar adds to the poet's is simply the inertia of their limited apprehension, which takes literally what he meant ideally, and degrades into a false extension of this world on its own level what in his mind was a true interpretation of it upon a moral plane.

This higher plane is the sphere of significant imagination, of relevant fiction, of idealism become the interpretation of the reality it leaves behind. Poetry raised to its highest power is then identical with religion grasped in its inmost truth; at their point of union both reach their utmost purity and beneficence, for then poetry loses its frivolity and ceases to demoralize, while religion surrenders its illusions and ceases to deceive.